Houghton Mifflin

Math

MATH Center

- **Teacher Notes**
- **Blackline Masters including**
  - Cross-Curricular Activities
  - Number Sense Activities
  - Workmats
  - Gameboards
  - Spinners
  - Card Decks

GRADE

1

Introduction to the Math Center

What Is the Math Center?

The Houghton Mifflin Math Center is a chapter-by-chapter resource book of hands-on games and activities that reinforce and deepen children's mathematics skills and concepts. These reproducible resources provide teachers with engaging ways to help children put math into practice.

How Do Teachers Use the Math Center?

The program is flexible—teachers can guide children through the activities or allow children to work independently. Activities are planned so children can work individually, in pairs, or in small groups. Games are structured for partners or small groups.

How Does the Math Center Enhance Learning?

The Math Center enhances learning by engaging children in immediate and relevant application of recently learned concepts and skills. Children are given ample and exciting practice through mathematical games, as well as through real-life, cross-curricular, and vocabulary activities. These participatory activities are designed to motivate children at all levels, from early finishers to those who may need to spend extra time on a concept.

Math Center Components

Activity Sheets

The Activity Sheets are designed to reinforce and consolidate learning. They list:

• clearly stepped-out instructions

• all necessary materials

• an interesting Try This! extension of the activity

So, whether children work on their own or in groups, they have the information they need to carry out the activity.

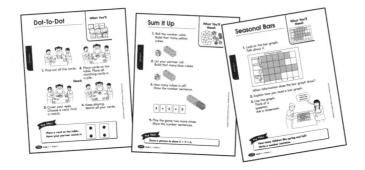

Number of the Week

The Number of the Week is a great way to help children think differently about mathematical ideas. For example, by considering a specific number as a quantity, measurement, and a term in a pattern, children begin to realize the interconnectedness of math ideas.

• Number of the Week activities cover Number Sense, Algebraic Thinking/Patterns, Data, Measurement, and Geometry.

• Every chapter in Houghton Mifflin Mathematics has a corresponding Number of the Week.

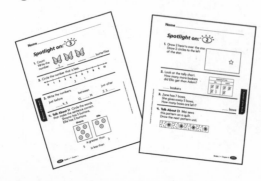

Teacher Notes

Your Teacher Notes provide an efficient and quick reference for any advance preparation and materials needed for each activity. The Teacher Notes also include:

• tips for modeling the activity in the classroom

• helpful hints for guiding children through an activity

• answers to questions in an activity

Resources

These reproducible gameboards, workmats, cards, spinners, graphs, calendars, and place-value charts can be used over and over again. Just use a counter (or any other small classroom object) as a game piece with a gameboard and you have an economical and fun way to help your children practice what they have just learned.

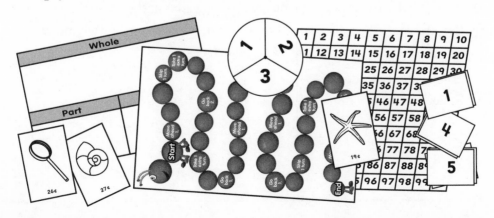

Tips on Organizing and Managing the Math Center

Here are some handy, teacher-created tips for making your Math Center both exciting and efficient.

Classroom Set-Up

If you have a small, free corner in your room, put up a child-made sign designating the Math Center. Your Math Center can be as compact as a cardboard box filled with file folders of the activities, or as ample as a table display of manipulative resources and activity sheets. Either way, it is your children's special math place.

Resources

When resources, gameboards, workmats, or cards are to be cut out and used for an activity, consider gluing them onto cardboard or file folders, or laminating them to increase their durability.

Organization

The Houghton Mifflin Math Center Unit Planners provide "at a glance" information that you will need for each activity.

One way to organize your Math Center is to create folders containing the materials for each activity. Then group activity folders together in a larger folder or box.

Materials

When an activity calls for game pieces or counters, use whatever is available—actual pieces from a game in the classroom, buttons, plastic bottle caps, or any other small objects.

Grouping

Some games can be played by partners as readily as by small groups, and some partner activities can be easily adapted for children to do on their own.

You can use color-coding on an activity as a reminder of how you've used an activity in the past. For example, blue might represent small groups and yellow might represent partner work.

Revisiting Activities

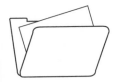

Revisiting activities or games and adapting them for new content and skills can help to build children's self-confidence. Since they already know the steps, or the rules, of the game, setup time is quicker, and time spent on the task is more meaningful.

Time Designations

The pacing for an activity is the average time needed for setup and play. However, the needs of your children may require increasing or decreasing the length of an activity.

An egg timer or a kitchen timer is a good way to help children keep track of how much time is remaining in an activity.

Preparation

Children's families and other volunteers can help prepare materials ahead of time. Once specific activity materials have been prepared, they can be stored and labeled with the activity name.

Suggested Alternatives to Program Manipulatives

HMMath Manipulatives	Suggested Alternatives
Attribute Blocks	seashells, pasta, buttons
Balance Scales	clothes hanger, paper cups, and string
Bill Set	bills made from construction paper and markers
Blank Number Cubes with Labels	number cards, spinners
Coin Set	real coins, buttons
Connecting Cubes	paper clips, string and beads or pasta
Counting Chips	buttons, coins, beans
Demonstration Clock	clock face with two lengths of string fastened to the center for hands
Geometric Solids	cans, boxes, balls, cones, modeling clay shapes
Pattern Blocks	shapes cut out of different-colored construction paper or cardboard
Place-Value Blocks	grid paper cutouts
Ruler, inch and centimeter	one-inch or one-centimeter grid paper strips
Transparent Spinner	construction paper, paper clip, and pencil
Two-Color Counters	coins, washers, or beans with one side painted

Table of Contents

Activities	Use After HMMath	Teacher Note	Student Page	Resource Pages
Chapter 21: Adding Two-Digit Numbers				
Tens and Tens	Lesson 21.1	p. 128	p. 198	
Roll into Place	Lesson 21.2	p. 128	p. 199	• Tens and Ones Workmat (pp. 288–289) • 4-Part Spinner (p. 278)
Pick and Spin	Lesson 21.3	p. 129	p. 200	• 4-Part Spinner (p. 278) • Number Cards 20–44 (pp. 264–266) • Tens and Ones Workmat (pp. 288–289) • Place-Value Sheet (p. 243)
Pick and Spin *Variation*	Lesson 21.4	p. 130		• 4-Part Spinner (p. 278) • Number Cards 20–44 (pp. 264–266) • Tens and Ones Workmat (pp. 288–289) • Place-Value Sheet (p. 243)
Roll Into Place Variation	Lesson 21.5	p. 130		• Tens and Ones Workmat (pp. 288–289) • 4-Part Spinner (p. 278)
Number of the Week Spotlight on 49	Lesson 21.6	p. 131	p. 224	
Chapter 22: Subtracting Two-Digit Numbers				
Take It Away	Lesson 22.1	p. 133		• Playing Card Master (p. 274)
Rolling Away	Lesson 22.2	p. 133	p. 201	• 6-Part Spinner (p. 279)
Number Boxes	Lesson 22.3	p. 134	p. 202	• Number Cards 1–50 (pp. 262–267) • Tens and Ones Workmat (pp. 288–289)
Rolling Away *Variation*	Lesson 22.4	p. 134		• 6-Part Spinner (p. 279)
Spin Away	Lesson 22.5	p. 135	p. 203	• 6-Part Spinner (p. 279)
Apart and Together	Lesson 22.6	p. 135		• Number Cards 45–59 (pp. 267–268) • 10-Part Spinner (p. 280) • Part-Part-Whole Workmat (pp. 284–285)
Number of the Week Spotlight on 36	Lesson 22.7	p. 136	p. 225	

Unit 1 Planner
Chapter 1

Use after . . .

LESSON 1.1

Towers Up

For each pair:
- Towers Up, p. 137
- Playing Card Master, p. 274
- blue connecting cubes
- yellow connecting cubes

LESSON 1.2

Dot-to-Dot

For each group:
- Dot-to-Dot, p. 138
- Dot Cards 1–9, p. 261 (4 copies)

LESSON 1.3

Chairs

For each pair:
- Chairs, p. 139
- Ten-Frame Sheet, p. 248
- Number Cards 1–20, pp. 262–264
- cubes

LESSON 1.4

Before or After

For each pair:
- 3-Column Chart, p. 227
- Number Cards 0–20, pp. 262–264
- Caterpillar Gameboard, pp. 290–291
- 2 gamepieces

LESSON 1.5

Towers Up
Variation

For each pair:
- Towers Up, p. 137
- Playing Card Master, p. 274
- blue connecting cubes
- yellow connecting cubes

LESSON 1.6

Show Your Number

For each pair:
- Number Cards 0–20, pp. 262–264 (2 copies)
- Number Lines, p. 240
- index cards
- counters

LESSON 1.7

Number of the Week Spotlight on 3

For each student:
- Spotlight on 3, p. 204

Chapter 1

USE AFTER LESSON 1.1

Towers Up

VOCABULARY

OBJECTIVE Compare sets using the terms *more, fewer,* and *same*

MANAGEMENT Pairs

TIME 15 minutes

MATERIALS PER PAIR
- Towers Up (p. 137)
- Playing Card Master (p. 274)
- blue connecting cubes
- yellow connecting cubes

Before the Activity

Build ten blue and ten yellow cube towers. Each tower has from one to ten cubes. Use the Playing Card Master (p. 274) to make 3 sets of vocabulary cards for *more, fewer,* and *same.*

Modeling the Activity

Display the cube towers and place the vocabulary cards in a pile facedown. Have a volunteer help you demonstrate. Hold up a blue tower. Ask: **How many cubes are in this tower? [8]** Now choose a card from the pile and read it aloud. Say: **Find a yellow tower with [fewer] cubes. Count how many.** Remind children they can place the two towers side by side to help them match the cubes one-to-one. Ask: **Does your tower have [fewer] than the blue tower?** Children take turns as they repeat the activity until all the cards have been used.

Be sure children understand that if a one-cube tower is chosen, then their partner will have to find *more* or *same.* If a ten-cube tower is chosen, then their partner will have to choose *less* or *same.*

Helpful Hint

If time allows, have one partner choose a tower and a card [less] and then have the partner find all the towers with [less].

USE AFTER LESSON 1.2

OBJECTIVE Count sets and find sets with the same number

MANAGEMENT Groups

TIME 15 minutes

MATERIALS PER GROUP
- Dot-to-Dot (p. 138)
- 4 copies of Dot Cards (p. 261)

Dot-to-Dot

Before the Activity

Make 4 copies of Dot Cards (p. 261) for each group.

Modeling the Activity

Display the cards face up. Have children count dots on some of the cards. Ask: **Are the number of dots the same?** Tell children they will match cards with the same number of dots.

Show two 2-dot cards and one 5-dot card. Ask: **Which cards have the same number of dots?**

Distribute the cards evenly to the group of children. Have each child place their cards face up in front of them. Say: **If you have two cards with the same number of dots, place them in a pile.** Ask: **How do you know the cards match?**

Choose a player to go first. Say: **Cover your eyes.** Guide the child to choose a card from the player to the right. Say: **Uncover your eyes. Do you have a card that has the same number of dots as the one you chose?** If the card does not match the child places it in front of them and the next player continues. Children take turns picking a card from the player to the right until one player matches all of his or her cards.

> **Helpful Hint**
>
> You may allow children to use counters to place on top of the dots as they count and match.

USE AFTER LESSON 1.3

OBJECTIVES Count objects to 20; relate written numbers to real world objects

MANAGEMENT Pairs

TIME 15 minutes

MATERIALS PER PAIR
- Chairs (p. 139)
- Ten Frame Sheet (p. 248)
- Number Cards 0–20 (pp. 262–264)
- cubes

Chairs

Before the Activity

Prepare Number Cards 0–20 (pp. 262–264). Place them facedown on the table. Copy the Ten Frame Sheet (p. 248) for each pair. Discuss different times when children may need to count objects to 20. For example: Jenna invited 18 children to her play. She needs to count 18 chairs. Allow children to give other examples.

Modeling the Activity

Have a volunteer help you demonstrate. Explain that you will use the ten frame to count the number of chairs needed for a concert. Say: **I will choose a card to find how many people are attending the concert.** Choose a card and say the number aloud. [14] Have your partner use one cube for every chair needed. Say: **Place one chair in each box to count to [14].** Then count to check. If the number is correct, write the number on a sheet of paper.

Partners take turns picking cards, creating a story and placing cubes on the ten frame.

Before or After

OBJECTIVE Order numbers 0–20 using the words *before* and *after*

MANAGEMENT Pairs

TIME 15 minutes

MATERIALS PER PAIR
- 3-Column Chart (p. 227)
- Number Cards 0–20 (pp. 262–264)
- Caterpillar Gameboard (pp. 290–291)
- 2 game pieces

Before the Activity

Prepare the 3-Column Chart (p. 227) with the labels *Before, Number,* and *After.* Copy Number Cards 0–20 (pp. 262–264) and the Caterpillar Gameboard (pp. 290–291) for pairs.

Modeling the Activity

Draw attention to the gameboard and review how to move around the board. Have a volunteer help you demonstrate the game. Mix the cards and place them facedown. Say: **Choose a card. Read the number. [12]** Point to the middle column and say: **Write the number on the chart.** Guide the child to write [12] in the middle column.

Before	Number	After
	12	

12

Then explain that the child will decide whether he or she wants the partner to write the number *before* or *after* the number on their card. Assume the child chooses *before* and say: **So I will write the number before [12].** Demonstrate writing the number [11] in the first column on the chart. Say: **Now I can move my game piece forward [11] spaces.** Return the card to the bottom of the deck. Partners switch roles and continue until each player reaches the End space on the gameboard. Tell children they do not have to get the exact number to land on the End space.

Helpful Hint

You may want to give pairs a copy of a 0–20 number line to help them identify before and after numbers.

USE AFTER LESSON 1.5

Towers Up
Variation

VOCABULARY

OBJECTIVES Compare two numbers 0–20; use the terms *greater than* and *less than*

Before the Activity

Repeat "Towers Up," as described in Lesson 1.1 (p. 12). Vary the activity by using the word cards *greater than* and *less than*. Build cube towers consisting of one to twenty cubes. Use Number Cards 0–50 (pp. 262–267).

Modeling the Activity

Play "Towers Up," but have children place their number cards on the table facedown. Have a child choose a tower. Say: **Count the cubes. Write the number. Now choose a number card.** Have the child tell whether the number of cubes in the tower is *greater than* or *less than* the number on the card. Have the child hold up the word card as they say the comparison aloud. For example: My tower has 12 cubes. My number card is 11. 12 is *greater than* 11.

USE AFTER LESSON 1.6

Show Your Number

VOCABULARY

OBJECTIVE Compare two numbers 0–20 using a number line

MANAGEMENT Pairs

TIME 15 minutes

MATERIALS PER PAIR
- 2 copies of Number Cards 0–20 (pp. 262–264)
- Number Lines (p. 240)
- index cards
- counters

Before the Activity

Make 2 copies of Number Cards 0–20 (pp. 262–264). Prepare two blank Number Lines 0–10 and 11–20 (p. 240). Label two index cards: *is greater than* and *is less than*.

Modeling the Activity

Have two volunteers demonstrate how to play the game. Have children cut out the number lines and place them side by side. Distribute the Number Cards evenly. Have each child mix their cards and place them in a pile facedown. Say: **Turn over the top card.** Have one partner choose a word [greater] and say: **Now you will find the [greater] number.**

 is greater than

Focus attention on the number lines. Say: **Find your number on the number line. Place a counter on the number.** Have the other partner use the two number cards and the word card to show which number is greater. Say: **Place the word card between the two numbers to show which is greater.** Instruct the child to say the comparison aloud. If the comparison is correct, the child takes both number cards. Partners switch roles and play until all the number cards have been used. If both players pick the same number, have them return the cards and each pick a new card.

USE AFTER LESSON 1.7

NUMBER OF THE WEEK
Spotlight on 3

NUMBER SENSE

OBJECTIVE Use the number 3 in problem-solving contexts

MANAGEMENT Individuals

TIME 15 minutes

MATERIALS
- Spotlight on 3 (p. 204)

Before the Activity

Make a copy of Spotlight on 3 (p. 204) for each child.

Modeling the Activity

Show children the Spotlight on 3 sheet. Say: **Today you will explore different ways to use the number 3.** Read the first activity and ask: **How many butterflies?** Have children count aloud as you demonstrate writing the number 3 on the board. Remind children to point to each butterfly as they count.

Give each child a copy of Spotlight on 3. Read the other exercises to the class. After each set of directions, give children time to complete the activity.

Answers

1. 3 butterflies
2. 1 is circled
3. 3; 13; 4
4. 5 is greater than 3

Unit 1 Planner
Chapter 2

Use after . . .

LESSON 2.1
Draw and Tell

For each pair:
- Draw and Tell, p. 140
- Story Mat, p. 244 (2 copies)
- 6 counters

LESSON 2.2
Shake and Spill

For each student:
- Shake and Spill, p. 141
- Part-Part-Whole Workmat, pp. 284–285
- Number Cards 5–6, p. 262
- six 2-sided counters
- cup

LESSON 2.3
Sum It Up

For each student:
- Sum It Up, p. 142
- Number Cards 1–6, p. 262 (2 sets)
- number cube
- 3 blue connecting cubes
- 3 yellow connecting cubes

LESSON 2.4
Just the Same

For each pair:
- Just the Same, p. 143
- Blank Spinner, p. 276
- 12 connecting cubes

LESSON 2.5
Domino Dynamos

For each pair:
- Domino Cards, pp. 258–260

LESSON 2.6
Add and Move

For each pair:
- Fan Gameboard, pp. 292–293
- large sheet of paper
- 2 number cubes
- 2 gamepieces

LESSON 2.7
Domino Dynamos
Variation

For each pair:
- Domino Cards, pp. 258–260

LESSON 2.8
Number of the Week Spotlight on 5

For each student:
- Spotlight on 5, p. 205

Chapter 2

USE AFTER LESSON 2.1

CROSS-CURRICULAR

OBJECTIVES Understand the concept of addition as increasing; create and act out addition stories

MANAGEMENT Pairs

TIME 15 minutes

MATERIALS PER PAIR
- Draw and Tell (p. 140)
- 2 copies of Story Mats (p. 244)
- 6 counters

Draw and Tell

Before the Activity

Make a copy of the Story Mat (p. 244) for each child. Show children the counters and explain that they stand for people in a story about a community. Help children brainstorm story settings, such as a park, a school, or a community center.

Modeling the Activity

Choose one of the story settings children suggest and sketch the scene on the Story Mat as children watch. Then, tell a brief story such as this: **Three children are cleaning up the playground.** Place three counters on the paper. Say: **Two of their friends stop to help.** Place two more counters on the paper. Ask: **Now how many children are cleaning the playground?**

Have children count the counters and tell how many people in all. Tell children they will make their own pictures and number stories to share with a partner.

Helpful Hint

Tell children they may draw any setting they like for their stories. Remind them that their stories should tell how many people and what they do.

USE AFTER LESSON 2.2

OBJECTIVE Illustrate a number as a whole, composed of different combinations of two other numbers (*parts*)

MANAGEMENT Individuals

TIME 15 minutes

MATERIALS
- Shake and Spill (p. 141)
- Part-Part-Whole Workmat (pp. 284–285)
- Number Cards 5–6 (p. 262)
- six 2-sided counters
- cup

Shake and Spill

Before the Activity

Make a copy of Shake and Spill (p. 141) and the Part-Part-Whole Workmat (pp. 284–285) for each child. Cut out Number Cards 5 and 6 (p. 262).

Modeling the Activity

Put a copy of the Part-Part-Whole Workmat on the table with the Number Card for 6, a cup, and six counters. Place the counters in the cup one at a time, counting each one aloud as you go. Emphasize the last number. Ask: **Who can tell me how many counters I put into the cup?** Give the cup a shake, and spill out the counters. Then ask how many of each color counters there are. Say, for example: **That's right. We started with six counters, then spilled out four red counters and two yellow counters.**

Show children the Part-Part-Whole Workmat. Place Number Card 6 at the top in the *whole* section. Then place the four red counters on one side and the two yellow counters on the other side. Point out that the Number Card shows all the counters, or the *whole*, and the left and right sides of the mat show the *parts.* Make sure children understand that by putting the parts together, they get the *whole*.

Give each child Number Cards 5 and 6, counters, Shake and Spill, and the Part-Part-Whole Workmat. Tell them to choose a Number Card to place at the top of the mat in the *whole* section. They should make sure they have that same number of counters in their cup before they shake and spill. Then they should put each color on the correct *part* side and add them together to get the *whole*.

USE AFTER LESSON 2.3

Sum It Up

VOCABULARY

OBJECTIVES Use *plus* and *equal* signs and the term *sum;* join two groups to find how many in all

MANAGEMENT Pairs

TIME 15 minutes

MATERIALS PER PAIR
- Sum It Up (p. 142)
- 2 sets of Number Cards 1–6 (p. 262)
- number cube
- 3 blue connecting cubes, 3 yellow connecting cubes

Before the Activity

For each pair of children, label a number cube with the numbers 1, 1, 2, 2, 3, and 3. Copy two sets of Number Cards 1–6 (p. 262) and the cards showing the *plus* and *equals* signs.

Modeling the Activity

Show children the blue and yellow connecting cubes. Have a volunteer roll the number cube. Say: **What number did you roll? Put that many yellow cubes together and place them on the table.**

Then have another volunteer roll the number cube and do the same with the blue cubes. Say: **Place your blue cubes next to the yellow cubes.**

Ask: **How many yellow cubes? How many blue cubes?** Have a child connect the yellow and blue cubes. Ask: **How many cubes in all?** Call on a volunteer to use Number Cards to show the number sentence and read it to the class. (For example, Three plus two equals five, or 3 + 2 = 5.) Say: **Another way to say that is, "The *sum* of three and two is five."**

Repeat the procedure, calling on volunteers to roll the number cube, join the cubes, and show the number sentence with cards. Be sure to have them read the sentence aloud.

Helpful Hint

As each child reads their number sentence, hold up the cards as they are read, to emphasize the connection between the word and the symbol.

USE AFTER
LESSON 2.4

Just the Same

OBJECTIVE Explore the role of zero in addition

MANAGEMENT Pairs

TIME 10 minutes

MATERIALS PER PAIR

- Just the Same (p. 143)

- Blank Spinner (p. 276)

- 12 connecting cubes

Before the Activity

Using the Blank Spinner (p. 276), make a spinner divided into halves labeled +0, +1. Give each child six cubes.

Modeling the Activity

Display six connecting cubes and let children count them. Put three of the cubes together to form a train. Say: **Start with a train of three cubes. The first player spins the spinner. Then the player does what the spinner says.** Display the spinner and spin it. Ask: **What does the spinner tell me to do?** Model responding to both directions by adding 1 and adding 0.

Then ask: **Does this cube train change when I add zero cubes? Does it change when I add one cube?** As children respond, model adding zero and one cube.

Explain that each player in a small group will begin with a 3-cube train and will take three turns with the spinner. To wrap up, say: **Look at your cube trains. How many cubes do you have in your train? Do any players still have exactly three cubes in their trains?**

Discuss with children examples in their lives when they add 0 or add 1. For example, if they invite a friend for lunch, they would add 1 sandwich to the total number of sandwiches. If they do not invite a friend, they would add 0.

Helpful Hint

Be sure that children are not adding any cubes when the spinner indicates +0.

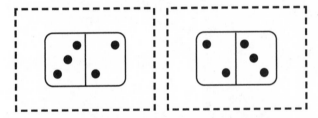

USE AFTER LESSON 2.5

OBJECTIVE Use the order property of addition to solve addition facts through six

MANAGEMENT Pairs

TIME 10 minutes

MATERIALS PER PAIR
- Domino Cards (pp. 258–260)

Domino Dynamos

Before the Activity

Remove all Domino Cards whose dots total more than six (both sides together). They will not be used in this activity.

Modeling the Activity

Show children a Domino Card and ask: **How many dots do you count on this side? How many do you count on the other side?** Say: **We will use these cards to play an addition game with partners. The game begins with all the Domino Cards spread out, facedown.** Say: **Now one player picks a Domino Card and turns it over. That player holds the card so the two sets of dots are side by side.** Show children how to hold the card. Point to the left side and ask a volunteer: **How many dots are on this side?** Point to the right side, and ask: **How many dots on this side? How many dots altogether? Can you say that in an addition sentence?** Model the addition sentence. For example, say: **Three plus two equals five.**

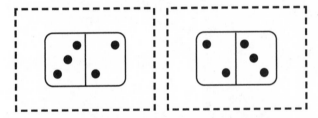

Say: **Now the other player turns the Domino Card around and adds the dots.** Ask another volunteer to help demonstrate. Make sure children understand that the sum is the same regardless of the order in which they are added together.

Instruct paired partners to take turns picking cards and adding the dots together.

Add and Move

OBJECTIVE Generate combinations of numbers with sums through 8

MANAGEMENT Pairs

TIME 15 minutes

MATERIALS PER PAIR
- Fan Gameboard (pp. 292–293)
- large sheet of paper
- 2 number cubes
- 2 game pieces

Before the Activity

Label the number cubes 0–4. On a large sheet of paper, prepare an answer sheet showing all possible combinations of rolls and sums for the two number cubes (0 + 0 = 0, 0 + 1 = 1, 0 + 2 = 2, and so on.) Display the answer sheet in the classroom. Draw a tree, house, car, or ball in the same order in each section of the fan.

Modeling the Activity

Display the Fan Gameboard (pp. 292–293). Point to the fans and say: **You and your partner will each sit in front of a fan and take turns rolling two number cubes. You add the numbers on your cubes and then move one space on your fan.**

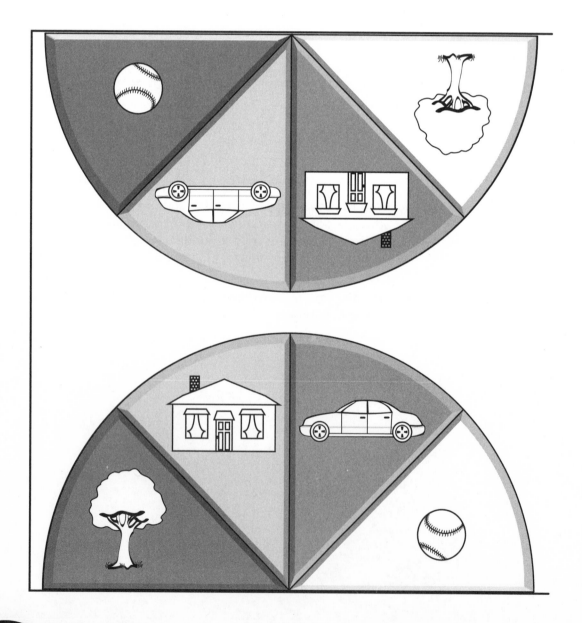

Ask two volunteers to demonstrate. Say: **Each section of your fan has a different picture.** Have partners each place their game piece on the tree space of their fan. Tell one child to roll the cubes. Ask: **What numbers are showing? Let's add them together. What is the sum? Let's check the answer sheet to see if you are correct. If you are, you may move your game piece to the next space on your fan. If your answer is not correct, you may not move your game piece and it's your partner's turn.** Help the second player take their turn.

Explain that once a player has moved all four spaces on the fan, then that player must roll a sum of 7 or 8 to "get off the gameboard." The game ends when the first player gets off the gameboard.

(**Helpful Hint**)

During the year, as children become familiar with the game, you might want to encourage them to play in groups of three or four.

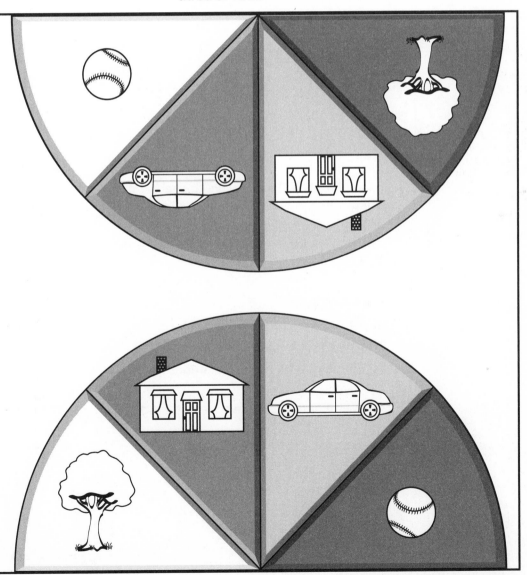

Domino Dynamos
Variation

OBJECTIVE Use the order property of addition to solve addition facts through 8

Modeling the Activity

Repeat "Domino Dynamos" (p. 21), as described in Lesson 2.5. Vary the activity by removing all Domino Cards whose dots total more than eight. Tell children that in this variation both players must write the addition sentence. One writes it horizontally, the other writes it vertically, and they compare sums. Hold up a Domino Card horizontally, then vertically, to show children how to write their addition problems, then write a sample addition sentence on the board.

Instruct paired partners to take turns picking cards and adding the dots together. Whoever picks the card writes vertically; the other partner writes horizontally.

NUMBER OF THE WEEK
Spotlight on 5

NUMBER SENSE

OBJECTIVE Use the number 5 in problem-solving contexts

MANAGEMENT Individuals

TIME 15 minutes

MATERIALS
• Spotlight on 5 (p. 205)

Before the Activity

Make a copy of Spotlight on 5 (p. 205) for each child.

Modeling the Activity

Give each child a copy of Spotlight on 5 sheet. Say: **You will be exploring different ways to use the number 5.** Read over the problems, and answer any questions children may have before they begin.

When all children have finished, review the answers with the class.

Answers

1. 5 bananas

2. $4 + 1 = 5$; 5 pancakes

3. The pentagon should be underlined.

4. 5 cubes; *Answers may vary. Sample:* I put 3 cubes together. Then I added 2 more cubes. José's crayon is 5 cubes long.

Unit 1 Planner
Chapter 3

Use after . . .

LESSON 3.1
Draw and Tell
Variation

For each pair:
- Draw and Tell, p. 140
- Story Mat, p. 244 (2 copies)
- 6 counters

LESSON 3.2
Missing Part Stories

For each pair:
- Missing Part Stories, p. 144
- Part-Part-Whole Workmat, pp. 284–285
- Number Cards 1–5, p. 262
- five 2-color counters
- cup

LESSON 3.3
Count and Take Away

For each pair:
- Count and Take Away, p. 145
- 3-Part Spinner, p. 277
- Number Cards 1–6, p. 262
- counters

LESSON 3.4
Picture This!

For each student:
- Picture This!, p. 146
- Number Cards 1–6, p. 262
- Story Mat, p. 244
- crayons

LESSON 3.5
Just the Same
Variation

For each pair:
- Just the Same, p. 143
- Blank Spinner, p. 276
- 12 connecting cubes

LESSON 3.6
Count and Take Away
Variation

For each pair:
- Count and Take Away, p. 145
- 3-Part Spinner, p. 277
- Number Cards 1–6, p. 262
- counters

LESSON 3.7
Take Some Away

For each pair:
- Take Some Away, p. 147
- Story Mat, p. 244

LESSON 3.8
Number of the Week Spotlight on 7

For each student:
- Spotlight on 7, p. 206

Chapter 3

USE AFTER LESSON 3.1

Draw and Tell
Variation

OBJECTIVES Create and act out subtraction stories; understand the meaning of subtraction

Repeat "Draw and Tell" following the directions as described in Lesson 2.1 (p. 140). Have children tell subtraction stories by drawing the setting for their story. If children are having difficulty with the subtraction, remind them to 'take away' the counters and place them to the side.

USE AFTER LESSON 3.2

Missing Part Stories

OBJECTIVE Illustrate the properties of subtraction

MANAGEMENT Pairs

TIME 15 minutes

MATERIALS PER PAIR
- Missing Part Stories (p. 144)
- Part-Part-Whole Workmat (pp. 284–285)
- Number Cards 1–5 (p. 262)
- five 2-color counters
- cup

Before the Activity

Make copies of Missing Part Stories (p. 144) and Part-Part-Whole Workmat (pp. 284–285) for each pair of children. Copy the Number Cards and pull out cards 1–5.

Modeling the Activity

Place five counters in the cup, saying: **I'm putting five 'apples' in this cup.** Put Number Card 5 at the top *whole* section of the Part-Part-Whole Mat.

Ask a volunteer to shake the cup, then reach in and take out three apples. Have them place the counters on one side of the Part-Part-Whole Workmat, red side up. Ask: **If we put five apples in the cup and take out three, how many apples are left?**

Ask another volunteer to spill the remaining two apples, placing them yellow side up on the other half of the Part-Part-Whole Workmat. Have him or her count the yellow apples and say the number out loud. Ask: **Can you tell a subtraction story about the apples?**

Allow time for partners to take turns spilling, counting, and telling a subtraction story.

USE AFTER
LESSON 3.3

Count and Take Away

OBJECTIVES Use minus and equal signs; separate a smaller set from a larger set to find how many are left

MANAGEMENT Pairs

TIME 15 minutes

MATERIALS PER PAIR
- Count and Take Away (p. 145)
- 3-Part Spinner (p. 277)
- Number Cards 1–6 (p. 262)
- counters

Before the Activity

Copy two 3-Part Spinners. Label one spinner 1, 2, 3. Label the other spinner 4, 5, 6. Make two copies of Number Cards 1–6. Sort out the 1–6 cards, and the minus and equal signs.

Modeling the Activity

Call on a volunteer to be your partner. Spin the 4–6 Spinner. Show the number and have children count along as you put out that many counters. Then ask your partner to spin the 1–3 Spinner. Say: **Now take away that many counters.** Have your partner slide that number of counters apart from the others. Ask: **How many counters are left?**

Model using the Number Cards, and the minus and equal cards to make a subtraction sentence.

Explain that partners will take turns, first spinning the 4–6 Spinner and then the 1–3 Spinner, and work together to show the subtraction sentences.

> **Helpful Hint**
>
> Make certain children always roll the 4–6 Spinner first so that they are able to subtract the second number.

USE AFTER
LESSON 3.4

Picture This!

OBJECTIVE Draw pictures and write subtraction sentences to solve subtraction problems to 6

MANAGEMENT Individuals

TIME 15 minutes

MATERIALS
- Picture This!
- Number Cards 1–6 (p. 262)
- Story Mat (p. 244)
- crayons

Before the Activity

Copy a Story Mat (p. 244) for each child. Copy and sort out cards 1–6 from the Number Cards.

Modeling the Activity

Show children the Number Cards. Display the card for 6 and explain that they will always be taking away from that number in this activity. Place the other cards facedown and turn over one card. Show the number and ask: **What number is this? Can we take this number away from six?**

Explain that you will draw a picture to show the subtraction from six. Draw a group of six stars. Tell this story: **One night I looked up and saw six bright stars.** Show the 6 card. Say: **Then a cloud came by. It covered this many stars.** Show the other card you picked. Cross out the number of stars that are covered by the cloud. Ask: **How many stars could I see in the beginning? How many of those stars are hidden? How many stars are left?** Write the subtraction sentence on the board, for example, 6 − [2] = [4].

Tell children they will use Story Mat to draw and solve another story problem. After they draw the story, they must write the subtraction sentence that tells what happened.

(Helpful Hint)

Reassure children that their pictures are not the focus of this problem. If they are having trouble drawing stars, encourage them to use dots and to show subtraction by crossing out the dots.

USE AFTER LESSON 3.5

OBJECTIVE Explore the role of zero in subtraction

Just the Same
Variation

Repeat "Just the Same" as described in Lesson 2.4 (p. 143). Vary the activity by preparing a 2-Part Spinner labeled *–0* and *–all*. Give each child 6 cubes.

Ask questions such as: **Does the cube train change when I subtract zero cubes? Does it change when I subtract all the cubes?** As children respond, model subtracting zero and all the cubes.

Explain that each player in a small group will begin with a 6-cube train, and will take two turns with the spinner. After two turns, ask: **Do any players still have six cubes in their trains? Do any players have no cubes left?** Have children write a subtraction sentence showing what they did. For example, 6 − 0 = 6, or 6 − 6 = 0.

USE AFTER LESSON 3.6

OBJECTIVE Separate a smaller set from a larger set to find how many are left

Count and Take Away
Variation

Repeat "Count and Take Away," as described in Lesson 3.3 (p. 145). Vary the activity by preparing 2 spinners, one with the numbers 1–4 and the other with the numbers 5–8. Use the Number Cards 1–8. Children write the number sentences.

Take Some Away

Teacher Notes

OBJECTIVES Use a picture to write a difference; recognize the vertical form of subtraction

MANAGEMENT Pairs

TIME 15 minutes

MATERIALS PER PAIR
• Take Some Away (p. 147)

• Story Mat (p. 244)

Before the Activity

Cover the writing lines at the bottom of the Story Mat (p. 244) and make one copy of Take Some Away (p. 147) for each child.

Modeling the Activity

Begin by saying: **Today we are going to make up number stories to tell a partner.** Hold up a Story Mat and point to the area inside the frame, saying: **Each of you will draw up to ten things here and make up a subtraction number story about the things you drew. You'll tell your partner the subtraction story. Then your partner will cross out the things that went away and write the number sentence two ways.**

Choose a volunteer partner to demonstrate. On a Story Mat, draw items such as nine sailboats, for example, and say: **One day I saw nine boats on the water. Then five of the boats sailed away.** Have your partner cross out the things that went away and write a horizontal and a vertical number sentence about it. Make sure the number sentences are visible to all students.

Let paired partners switch tasks as they play—one draws up to ten items and tells a number story; the other crosses out items and writes the corresponding number sentences.

Helpful Hint

Remind children to write the subtraction sentence two ways.

USE AFTER
LESSON 3.8

NUMBER OF THE WEEK
Spotlight on 7

NUMBER SENSE

OBJECTIVE Use the number 7 in problem-solving contexts

MANAGEMENT Individuals

TIME 15 minutes

MATERIALS
• Spotlight on 7 (p. 206)

Before the Activity

Make a copy of Spotlight on 7 (p. 206) for each child.

Modeling the Activity

Show children Spotlight on 7. Explain that they will be exploring different ways to use the number 7. Read the four problems and answer any questions children may have before they begin.

Give each child a copy of the Spotlight on 7 sheet. When all children have finished, review the answers with the class.

Answers

1. 1

2.
$$\begin{array}{r} 3 \\ + 4 \\ \hline 7 \end{array} \quad 3 + 4 = 7$$

3. The box with seven crayons should be circled.

4. 5 eggs are left because $7 - 2 = 5$.

Unit 1 Planner
Chapter 4

Use after . . .

LESSON 4.1
Tally Ho!

For each student:
- Tally Ho!, p. 148
- 3-Column Chart, p. 227
- cubes

LESSON 4.2
Get the Picture?
Cross-Curricular

For each pair:
- Get the Picture?, p. 149
- index cards

LESSON 4.3
Pet Survey
Vocabulary

For each student:
- Pictograph, p. 242

LESSON 4.4
Seasonal Bars
Cross-Curricular

For each group:
- Seasonal Bars, p. 150

LESSON 4.5
Favorite Fruit Survey

For each student:
- Favorite Fruit Survey, p. 151
- Bar Graph (4-Row), p. 233
- crayons

LESSON 4.6
**Number of the Week
Spotlight on 8**

For each student:
- Spotlight on 8, p. 207

Chapter 4

USE AFTER LESSON 4.1

OBJECTIVE Use tally marks to count

MANAGEMENT Individuals

TIME 10 minutes

MATERIALS
- Tally Ho! (p. 148)
- 3-Column Chart (p. 227)
- cubes

Tally Ho!

Before the Activity

Prepare groups of 25 cubes in 3 colors. Make a tally chart using the 3-Column Chart (p. 227) and labeling each column one of the cube colors.

Modeling the Activity

Have children count one group of cubes along with you. Tell children they will record how many cubes of each color there are on a tally chart. Have a volunteer help you demonstrate how to make a tally chart. Say: **Pick up one cube at a time.** Say: **One [green]** for each cube as you move it away from the group. Explain that you will mark a tally mark in the correct column after each time. Continue until you have five of any color. Say: **How do I group 5 tally marks?** Demonstrate using the diagonal line for the fifth mark. Remind children that the fifth mark makes it easy to identify groups of 5. Continue tallying the cubes until they have all been counted.

Now write how many cubes of each color are on the chart. Say: **Count the tally marks in the first column. Write how many at the bottom of the column.** Continue until the three columns have been counted. Ask: **Which color has the most? the fewest?** Allow time for children to share their tally charts.

USE AFTER LESSON 4.2

CROSS-CURRICULAR Social Studies

OBJECTIVE Interpret a picture graph

MANAGEMENT Pairs

TIME 15 minutes

MATERIALS PER PAIR
- Get the Picture? (p. 149)
- index cards

Get the Picture?

Before the Activity

Copy Get the Picture? (p. 149) for each pair. Prepare an index card for each toy on the graph. Place them in a pile.

Modeling the Activity

Display the Get the Picture? sheet. Focus attention on the graph and ask: **What does the information on the picture graph tell you?** Guide the children to read the title and look at the pictures.

Point to the stick figures on the picture graph. Ask: **What does each stick figure stand for?** Now point to the yo-yo and ask: **How many children chose a yo-yo as their favorite toy?** Then point to the car and ask: **How many children chose a car?** Now ask: **Did more children choose a yo-yo or a car?** Remind children to count one figure for each child.

Now have children mix their cards and place them facedown. Have one partner turn over the top two cards. Guide him or her to use the pictograph and pose a question to the other partner comparing information. When the partner answers, have children switch roles and continue.

Pet Survey

USE AFTER
LESSON 4.3

VOCABULARY

OBJECTIVE Make a pictograph of survey results

MANAGEMENT Individuals

TIME 15 minutes

MATERIALS
• Pictograph (p. 242)

Before the Activity

Prepare a copy of Pictograph (p. 242) with the following rebus and word labels: *cat, dog, bird, fish.* Title the graph: *Favorite Animals.* Copy a blank picture graph sheet to use as a tally chart.

Modeling the Activity

Hold up the picture graph and the tally chart. Tell children they will use the tally chart to gather information and then record the information on the graph. Say: **Look at the pets on the graph. We are going to find which pet is the favorite.** Explain to children that you will help them start the graph, but that they will complete the graph on their own.

Tell children you will begin by gathering information. Say: **Raise your hand when I name the pet that is your favorite.** Ask: **How many choose the dog as their favorite? cat? bird? fish?** Remind children to raise their hand only once. Ask a volunteer to help you count responses. Have another volunteer make tally marks for each response.

Now say: **Look at the tally chart. How many children chose the dog as a favorite animal? Count the marks in that row.** Point to the marks as children count aloud. Say: **Now draw that number of smiley faces in the same row on the picture graph.** Demonstrate drawing a small smiley face. Have children complete their graphs. Allow time for children to share their picture graphs.

Helpful Hint

Make sure children understand that each symbol (smiley face) stands for a child, not for an animal.

CROSS-CURRICULAR
Science

OBJECTIVE Interpret a
bar graph

MANAGEMENT Groups

TIME 15 minutes

MATERIALS PER GROUP
• Seasonal Bars (p. 150)

Seasonal Bars

Modeling the Activity

Display Seasonal Bars (p. 150). Discuss how a bar graph helps
you record and compare information. Read the title of the
graph. Ask: **What information does the bar graph show?**
Have children point to each season on the graph as you read
them aloud.

Ask: **How can we find out how many children chose spring?**
Have children explain that you start by finding spring on the
graph, then you follow the bar to the end, and drag a finger
to the number on the bottom of the graph. Four children
chose spring.

Have the children use the graph to think of questions that
compare the information.

OBJECTIVE Make a bar
graph of survey results

MANAGEMENT Individuals

TIME 15 minutes

MATERIALS
• Favorite Fruit Survey
  (p. 151)

• 4-Row Bar Graph (p. 233)

• crayons

Favorite Fruit Survey

Before the Activity

On the 4-Row Bar Graph (p. 233), draw small pictures of the
four fruits: banana, apple, watermelon slice, and grapes.
Make a copy for each child.

Modeling the Activity

Display the Favorite Fruit Survey (p. 151). Explain to the
children that you will help them start the bar graph, but they
will complete the bar graph on their own. Point to the tally
chart on the Favorite Fruit Survey and ask: **What information
does the tally chart show?** Then say: **You can make a bar
graph as another way to show the same information about
favorite fruits.**

Distribute the bar graph and say: **Look at the graph. What
title will you use?** Point to the title line and say: **Write your
title.** Remind children that they need to label the graph so
others can understand the information on the graph. Ask:
What labels will you write on the bottom and the side? Now
direct attention to Step 3. Ask: **How many children chose
apples? Color the bar on your graph to show that 5 children
chose apples.** Then say: **Use the tally chart. Complete the bar
graph on your own.** Allow time for children to discuss their
completed graphs.

Helpful Hint

Help children brainstorm a list of survey questions to ask each
other for the *Try This!* activity.

NUMBER OF THE WEEK
Spotlight on 8

NUMBER SENSE

OBJECTIVE Use the number 8 in problem-solving contexts

MANAGEMENT Individuals

TIME 15 minutes

MATERIALS
• Spotlight on 8 (p. 207)

Before the Activity

Make a copy of Spotlight on 8 (p. 207) for each child.

Modeling the Activity

Give each child a copy of Spotlight on 8. Say: **Today we will explore different ways to use the number 8**. Read the first activity and ask: **Do you add or subtract to find how many in all?** Have a volunteer explain how they will add to find how many in all.

Give each child a copy of Spotlight on 8. Read the other exercises to the class. After each set of directions, give children time to complete the exercise before moving on to the next set of directions.

Answers

1. 11 shapes

2. Shira

3. 8 children, 3 children

4. 3 more children like orange juice than grape juice because $8 - 5 = 3$.

Unit 2 Planner
Chapter 5

Use after . . .

LESSON 5.1
How Many?

For each pair:
- How Many?, p. 152
- Number Cards 4–7, p. 262
- ten 2-sided counters

LESSON 5.2
Line Up Facts

For each student:
- Line Up Facts, p. 153
- Addition Facts Through 12, p. 229
- Number Lines, p. 240

LESSON 5.3
Twice as Nice

For each group:
- Blank Spinner, p. 276
- Caterpillar Gameboard, pp. 290–291
- 2 counters

LESSON 5.4
Fill the Frame

For each student:
- 10-Part Spinner, p. 280
- Ten Frame Sheet, p. 248
- 10 connecting cubes of one color
- 10 connecting cubes of another color
- crayons to match the colors of the cubes

LESSON 5.5
Number of the Week
Spotlight on 6

For each student:
- Spotlight on 6, p. 208

Chapter 5

USE AFTER LESSON 5.1

OBJECTIVE Count on by 1, 2, and 3 to solve addition facts through 10

MANAGEMENT Pairs

TIME 15 minutes

MATERIALS PER PAIR
- How Many? (p. 152)
- Number Cards 4–7 (p. 262)
- plastic cup
- ten 2-sided counters

How Many?

Before the Activity

Copy the Number Cards and pull out the numbers 4–7.

Modeling the Activity

Put the Number Cards facedown in a pile. Call on a volunteer to pick a card and put it in front of the cup. For example, if the child picks a card with a 5 on it, say to a second volunteer: **Put five counters in the cup. Now pick up three more counters.** Ask the first child: **If we put these three more counters into the cup, how many counters will there be in the cup? How do you know?** Explain that you can count on from five because you know there are five counters in the cup already. Count aloud with children, saying: **6, 7, 8** as the child drops the other three counters into the cup.

Have pairs of children repeat the activity, using different Number Cards and adding 1, 2, or 3 counters each time.

> **Helpful Hint**

Remind children to empty the cup after each round of counting.

USE AFTER LESSON 5.2

OBJECTIVE Use a number line and other strategies to add facts through 10

MANAGEMENT Individuals

TIME 15 minutes

MATERIALS
- Line Up Facts (p. 153)
- Addition Facts Through 12 (p. 229)
- Number Lines (p. 240)

Line Up Facts

Before the Activity

Copy and cut apart the Addition Facts Cards (p. 229) through 12 to create a set for each child. (Only use cards where one addend is 1, 2, or 3.) Cover the numbers *11* and *12* on the top two Number Lines (p. 240) and label the three Blank Number Lines from 0 to 10. Make a copy for each child.

Modeling the Activity

Show the Number Line and a fact card with an addition problem such as

$$\begin{array}{r} 3 \\ + 5 \\ \hline \end{array}$$

Read the problem aloud. Say: **We can use a number line to help solve this problem.** Point to the first Number Line.

Ask: **Where should I start?** Remind children they should always start at zero. Say: **I have my finger on zero. I must always remember to jump to the higher of the two numbers** before I add. I will jump to 5. Jump to the five with your finger, then draw a pencil line from zero to five.

Ask: **How many do I count on?** With your finger, count three spaces from five, then mark it with a pencil.

Ask: **What number did I reach?** Call on a volunteer to write the number sentence $3 + 5 = 8$ right below the first Number Line.

Choose another fact card and model the process once more. Then have individual children pick three other cards and solve their problems, using the remaining Number Lines. Remind them to write the addition sentences below each line.

Helpful Hint

Have children use a finger to count on the Number Line before they mark it with their pencils.

USE AFTER LESSON 5.3

Twice as Nice

OBJECTIVE Solve doubles for facts through 10

MANAGEMENT Groups

TIME 15 minutes

MATERIALS PER GROUP
- Blank Spinner (p. 276)

- Caterpillar Gameboard (pp. 290–291)

- 2 counters

Before the Activity

Prepare an answer sheet showing all double combinations along with the sums: $1 + 1 = 2$, $2 + 2 = 4$, $3 + 3 = 6$, $4 + 4 = 8$, $5 + 5 = 10$. Copy it for children's use. Label a Blank Spinner (p. 276) 1, 2, 3, 4, 5. For each round, two children will play and a third child will be the checker.

Modeling the Activity

Show children the Caterpillar Gameboard (pp. 290–291). Say: **The object of this game is to move your counter from the start** (point to Start space) **to the end** (point to the End space). Have the first player spin the Spinner. Ask: **What number is showing? If you double that number, what is the sum?**

Have the player explain how he or she arrived at the sum. Have the third child in the group, the "checker," check the first player's answer, using the answer sheet. Say: **If your answer is correct, you may move your counter that many spaces on the gameboard. If your answer is not correct, you may not move your counter.**

Repeat the process with the second player. When one game is complete, the winner becomes the next checker. Play rotates until each child has had a chance to be the checker.

Fill the Frame

OBJECTIVE Use a Ten Frame to find combinations for sums of 10

MANAGEMENT Individuals

TIME 15 minutes

MATERIALS

- 10-Part Spinner (p. 280)
- Ten-Frame Sheet (p. 248)
- 10 connecting cubes of one color, 10 connecting cubes of another color
- crayons to match the colors of the cubes

Before the Activity

Label the 10-Part Spinner (p. 280) 1–10. Make two copies of the Ten-Frame Sheet for each child. Hand out two colors of cubes. Make sure children have matching colors of crayons.

Modeling the Activity

Have a child spin the 10-Part Spinner. Pointing to the number indicated by the spinner, say, for example: **Take that number of blue cubes. Put the cubes on one of the Ten Frames on the Ten-Frames Mat, one cube per square.** After the child does so, ask: **How many more cubes do you need to make 10? Take that many yellow cubes. Put the yellow cubes on the Ten Frame, one cube per square. Fill the frame.**

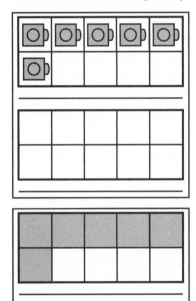

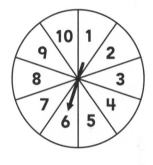

Have children color the other Ten-Frames Mat to match their workmat activity. Then say: **Write the number sentence that tells what you did.**

(**Helpful Hint**)

If you wish to have children practice with zero as an addend, make a rule that if the spinner lands on a line, the line represents zero.

Number of the Week
Spotlight on 6

NUMBER SENSE

OBJECTIVE Use the number 6 in problem-solving contexts

MANAGEMENT Individuals

TIME 15 minutes

MATERIALS
• Spotlight on 6 (p. 208)

Before the Activity

Make a copy of Spotlight on 6 (p. 208) for each child.

Modeling the Activity

Show children Spotlight on 6. Explain that they will be exploring different ways to use the number 6. Read over the four problems and answer any questions children may have before they begin.

Give each child a copy of Spotlight on 6. When all children have finished, review the answers with the class.

Answers

1. 6 children

2. 6 raindrops; 6 tally marks

3. 6 teeth

4. 6; *Answers will vary. Sample:* It is easier to start with the larger number 6 and count on 1.

Unit 2 Planner
Chapter 6

Use after . . .

LESSON 6.1
Back Down

For each student:
- Back Down, p. 154
- 4-Part Spinner, p. 278

LESSON 6.2
Along the Line

For each pair:
- Along the Line, p. 155
- Number Lines, p. 240
- 6-Part Spinner, p. 279
- 2 counters

LESSON 6.3
Spin and Win

For each pair:
- Blank Spinner, p. 276
- connecting cubes
- four 2-sided counters

LESSON 6.4
Roll It Out
Cross-Curricular

For each pair:
- Part-Part-Whole Workmat, pp. 284–285
- Part-Part-Whole Sheet, p. 241
- blank number cube
- 10 counters

LESSON 6.5
Family Fun

For each pair:
- Family Fun, p. 156
- Number Cards 1–9, +, −, and =; pp. 262–263, p. 267 (4 sets)

LESSON 6.6
Double Duty

For each pair:
- Domino Cards, pp. 258–260
- Caterpillar Gameboard, pp. 290–291
- 2 gamepieces

LESSON 6.7
Number of the Week Spotlight on 9

For each student:
- Spotlight on 9, p. 209

Chapter 6

OBJECTIVES Count back 1, 2 and 3; solve subtraction facts through 10

MANAGEMENT Individuals

TIME 15 minutes

MATERIALS
- Back Down (p. 154)
- Blank Spinner (p. 276)

Back Down

Before the Activity

Make a Spinner (p. 276) divided into quarters and labeled 0–3.

Modeling the Activity

Show children the spinner and say: **We're going to use the spinner to play a game counting back from 10 to zero.** Call on a volunteer to demonstrate as you explain. Say: **First write the number 10 on your paper. Now spin the spinner. What number did you spin?** After the volunteer responds, say, for example: **Yes, you spun 1 so count back 1.** Encourage children to start with 10 and count back 1 as the volunteer counts, saying: **10, 9. Now write 9 below the 10 on your paper.**

Then say: **This time when you spin, you'll count back from the last number on your paper.** Point out the number the volunteer wrote below the 10. Have the volunteer spin again. Again, encourage children to start with the last number on their paper and count back.

Explain that when children do the activity on their own, they will continue until they reach zero or until they cannot subtract the number they spin.

Helpful Hint

Make sure children count back from the number they recorded on their last turn.

OBJECTIVE Use a number line and other strategies to subtract with facts through 10

MANAGEMENT Pairs

TIME 15 minutes

MATERIALS PER PAIR
- Along the Line (p. 155)
- Number Lines (p. 240)
- 2 Blank Spinners (p. 276)
- 2 counters

Along the Line

Before the Activity

Label a blank number line on the Number Line sheet (p. 240) from 1–10, then copy. Label one Spinner (p. 276) 1, 1, 2, 2, 3, 3, and one 5–10.

Modeling the Activity

Display the Number Line. Say: **Look at this number line. In this game you'll use the number line to solve subtraction problems.**

Have the first player spin the 5–10 spinner. Ask: **What number did you spin? Put your counter above that number.**

Then have a second player spin the 1–3 spinner. Ask: **What number did you spin? Move the counter back that many numbers on the number line.**

Demonstrate for the child how to move the counter to the left. Ask: **What number is the counter on now?**

Ask the first player to write a subtraction sentence showing the moves. For example, if the first player spins 10 and the second player spins 3, the subtraction sentence would be 10 − 3 = 7.

Have the children reverse roles and continue playing.

Helpful Hint

Be sure the children spin the 5–10 spinner first to make sure they can count back.

USE AFTER LESSON 6.3

OBJECTIVE Subtract to compare groups

MANAGEMENT Pairs

TIME 15 minutes

MATERIALS PER PAIR
- Blank Spinner (p. 276)
- connecting cubes
- Four 2-sided counters

Spin and Win

Before the Activity

Use the Blank Spinner (p. 276) to make a spinner divided in half. Label one half "more" and label the other half "fewer."

Modeling the Activity

Show the connecting cubes. Have a volunteer build four towers of different heights, from five to ten cubes high, as you do the same. When the towers are made, ask: **How many cubes are in each tower?**

Choose one of your towers and have the volunteer choose one of his or hers. Place the two towers side by side and help children compare them. Ask: **Which tower has more cubes? How many more? Which tower has fewer cubes? How many fewer?**

Display the spinner and let children read the words *more* and *fewer*. Show the counters; explain that the spinner will show which player earns a counter—the one whose tower has more or fewer cubes. Spin the spinner. If the spinner shows more, ask: **Which tower has more cubes? How many more?**

Grade 1 • Chapter 6 **43**

Who gets the counter? If the spinner shows fewer, ask: **Which tower has fewer cubes? How many fewer? Who gets the counter?** Be sure children understand that they will not know whether the taller or the shorter tower gets the counter until they use the spinner.

Explain that children will make more comparisons and earn more counters with the other towers.

USE AFTER LESSON 6.4

Roll It Out

CROSS-CURRICULAR
Social Studies

OBJECTIVE Develop number sense by solving addition and subtraction problems through 10

MANAGEMENT Pairs

TIME 15 minutes

MATERIALS PER PAIR
• Part-Part-Whole Workmat (pp. 284–285)

• blank number cube

• 10 counters

Before the Activity

Label a number cube 0–5. Make a 3-Column Chart on the board labeled: *Guests, Milk,* and *Apple Juice.* Discuss with children the many different ways restaurant owners use addition and subtraction. For example: making recipes; setting tables for a number of guests; how many of each meal ordered, etc.

Modeling the Activity

Display the Part-Part-Whole Workmat (pp. 284–285) and the counters. Explain to children that they will create related addition and subtraction stories about a restaurant. Have a volunteer roll the number cube [3]. Say: **Place [3] counters in a Part section of the mat.** Write *3* under the *Milk* column on the board. Say: **[3] children ordered milk.** Now have the child roll the number cube again [5]. Say: **Place [5] counters in the other Part section of the mat.** Ask: **How many children ordered apple juice?** Write [5]. Show the Part-Part-Whole Workmat.

Say: **Now write the numbers on the Part-Part-Whole Workmat (pp. 283–284).** Ask: **How many counters do you have in all? Write this number in the Whole section.** Tell children this is how many children in all at the restaurant. Write [8] on the chart.

Now demonstrate how to write the addition sentence on the mat. Write each number as you say: **3 children ordered milk** *plus* **5 children ordered apple juice** *equals* **8 children in all. 3 + 5 = 8.** Now tell children you are going to write the related subtraction. Say: **5 children have finished their drinks. The waitress takes [5] glasses off the table. How many more glasses are still on the table?** Demonstrate writing 8 − 5 = 3. Remind children to use the counters on the mat to help them model the story problem. Continue with other related stories.

USE AFTER
LESSON 6.5

VOCABULARY

OBJECTIVE Complete a family of facts

MANAGEMENT Pairs

TIME 15 minutes

MATERIALS PER PAIR
- Family Fun (p. 156)
- 4 sets of Number Cards 1–9, +, − and = cards

Family Fun

Before the Activity

Mix one set of Number Cards 1–5 (p. 262) and place them facedown. Fan the rest of the cards face up.

Modeling the Activity

Call on two volunteers to turn over one card each from the facedown set and tell which number they picked. Say, for example: **Jeremy turned over a 4, and Malaika turned over a 5.** Put down a plus sign and finish the addition sentence. Guide the volunteers in selecting the appropriate cards from the face up pile to show the addition sentence, (for example: 4 + 5 = 9).

Then ask: **How can you show that addition sentence another way?** Help children select the same numbers and the other plus and equal signs to show the other addition fact, (5 + 4 = 9).

Show the minus sign and say: **Now use the same numbers and show the subtraction sentences.** Guide children in showing the subtraction sentences (9 − 4 = 5 and 9 − 5 = 4). Have pairs of children complete the activity with different numbers.

Helpful Hint

Remind children that in a fact family the same whole and parts are in all four facts.

OBJECTIVE Work with doubles in subtraction

MANAGEMENT Pairs

TIME 15 minutes

MATERIALS PER PAIR
- Domino Cards (pp. 258–260)
- Caterpillar Gameboard (pp. 290–291)
- 2 game pieces

Double Duty

Before the Activity

Select the doubles cards, facts to 10, from two sets of Domino Cards (pp. 258–260). Mix and place facedown.

Modeling the Activity

Display the Caterpillar Gameboard (pp. 290–291). Say: **The object of this game is to move your game piece from the Start space to the End space.**

Call on two volunteers to help demonstrate how the game is played. Show the Domino Card with five dots on each half. Say: **This is a doubles card. It has the same number of dots on both halves. What addition double does it make?** Then ask: **What subtraction double can you make with these numbers?**

Begin the game by having the first player pick a card. Ask: **What subtraction fact can you make from the card?**

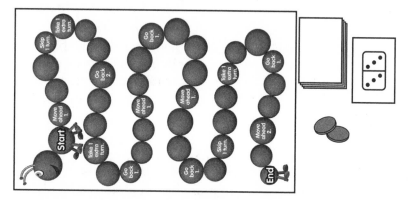

If the answer is correct, the player moves the same number of spaces as the answer to the subtraction fact. If the answer is incorrect, the player does not move. Players take turns until one reaches End.

Helpful Hint

Children may need to reshuffle the Domino Cards in order to complete the game.

NUMBER OF THE WEEK
Spotlight on 9

NUMBER SENSE

OBJECTIVE Use the number 9 to solve problems in many contexts

MANAGEMENT Individuals

TIME 15 minutes

MATERIALS
- Spotlight on 9 (p. 209)

Modeling the Activity

Show children Spotlight on 9 (p. 209) sheet. Say: **Today we will explore some other ways you can use the number 9.** Read the first activity and have a volunteer name out the numbers that are greater than 9. Then have children circle the numbers.

Read the directions for the other activities to the class. After each set of directions, give children time to complete the exercise before moving to the next set of directions.

Helpful Hint

Ask volunteers to share their solutions for Exercise 4. Children should realize that a triangle has three sides, so they can make a total of three triangles with nine sticks.

Answers

1. 12; 18; 10

2. 8; 7; 6

3. Children should circle the second set of tally marks.

4. 3 triangles

Unit 3 Planner
Chapter 7

Use after . . .

LESSON 7.1	**LESSON 7.2**	**LESSON 7.3**	**LESSON 7.4**
Something in Common	**Draw the Twin**	**Sorting Sets**	**Face to Face**
For each pair: • Sorting Cards, p. 275	For each pair: • Draw the Twin, p. 157 • Geoboard Dot Paper, p. 237	For each pair: • Playing Card Master, p. 274 • attribute blocks	For each student: • Face to Face, p. 158 • 3-Column Chart, p. 227 • geometric solid shapes (cube, cone, cylinder, rectangular prism, sphere, pyramid)

LESSON 7.5	**LESSON 7.6**	**LESSON 7.7**	
Face to Face *Variation*	**Shape Art** *Cross-Curricular*	**Number of the Week Spotlight on 4**	
For each student: • Face to Face, p. 158 • 3-Column Chart, p. 227 • geometric solid shapes (cube, cone, cylinder, rectangular prism, sphere, pyramid)	For each pair: • pictures of Cubist paintings • geometric solids • tracing paper • construction paper • paste • scissors	For each student: • Spotlight on 4, p. 210 • geometric solid shapes set	

Chapter 7

USE AFTER LESSON 7.1

OBJECTIVE Explore classifying objects by attributes

MANAGEMENT Pairs

TIME 15 minutes

MATERIALS PER PAIR
• Sorting Cards (p. 275)

Something in Common

Before the Activity

Prepare Sorting Cards (p. 275) for each pair.

Modeling the Activity

Display the Sorting Cards on the table and gather children to examine the item on each card. Ask: **How are the items alike?** Write the responses on the board. Tell children they will be sorting the cards into two groups. Have one volunteer choose a sorting rule. Ask: **How can we sort the items on the cards?** Have another volunteer sort the cards following the rule.

Then have pairs take turns choosing a sorting rule and sorting the cards into groups. Partners can collect the cards and repeat the activity until they have run out of possible ways to sort the items.

Helpful Hint

Encourage children to name the sorting rule and the attribute in each card to help them sort correctly.

USE AFTER LESSON 7.2

VOCABULARY

OBJECTIVE Identify and draw plane shapes of the same shape and size

MANAGEMENT Pairs

TIME 15 minutes

MATERIALS PER PAIR
• Draw the Twin (p. 157)

• Geoboard Dot Paper (p. 237)

Draw the Twin

Before the Activity

Make a copy of Geoboard Dot Paper (p. 237) for each child. Display the Draw the Twin (p. 157) sheet and a set of attribute blocks.

Modeling the Activity

Use the attribute blocks to review plane shapes. Hold up a square and have a volunteer identify and describe the shape. Ask: **How many sides and corners does it have?** Repeat with other shapes.

Then focus attention on the Draw the Twin sheet and the Geoboard Dot Paper. Tell children to cover their eyes as you draw a shape. Draw a square that is three dots high and three dots wide on your paper. Conceal the shape from children. Now tell children you want them to draw a 'twin' shape on their paper. Say: **Listen to my clues. Draw the shape. The shape is three dots high. It is three dots wide. The shape has four sides. The sides are the same length.**

When children have completed their drawings, hold up your paper and ask: **Is your shape a 'twin' of my drawing? What shape is it?** Have children compare their shapes and revise their drawings if necessary. Pairs take turns drawing and matching shapes.

USE AFTER LESSON 7.3

OBJECTIVE Classify and sort plane shapes

MANAGEMENT Pairs

TIME 15 minutes

MATERIALS PER PAIR
- Playing Card Master (p. 274)
- attribute blocks

Sorting Sets

Before the Activity

Use the Playing Card Master (p. 274) to prepare a set of playing cards for each pair. Cards should read as follows: *more than 2 sides, 3 sides, 4 sides, 4 sides the same, no corners, more than 2 corners, 3 corners,* and *4 corners.*

Modeling the Activity

Review the term *sorting rule.* Display the attribute blocks. Tell children they will choose a sorting rule and match shapes to the rule. Have children read aloud each sorting rule. Mix up the cards and place them facedown in an array. Focus attention on the attribute blocks. Choose a shape. Say: **How many sides does the shape have? How many corners?** Have volunteers describe other shapes in the same way.

Now have a child turn over one card. Ask: **What is the sorting rule?** Have the child read the card. Say: **Find all the shapes that follow the sorting rule.**

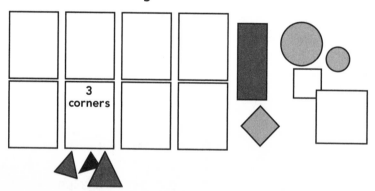

Guide the child in sorting the shapes according to the rule. When all shapes have been identified, have the child put the shapes back into the pile and turn over the next card. Have pairs take turns reading the rule and matching the shapes until all the cards have been turned over.

If time allows, you may want the children to find objects in the classroom that follow each rule.

USE AFTER
LESSON 7.4

OBJECTIVE Identify, describe, and sort solid shapes

MANAGEMENT Individuals

TIME 10 minutes

MATERIALS
- Face to Face (p. 158)
- 3-Column Chart (p. 227)
- geometric solid shapes (cube, cone, cylinder, rectangular prism, sphere, pyramid)

Face to Face

Before the Activity

Prepare ten 2" × 1" labels on index cards as follows: *1 face, 8 corners, 12 edges, 0 faces, 5 faces, 8 edges, 6 faces, 2 faces, 0 corners, 5 corners.* Make a copy of the 3-Column Chart (p. 227) and display it with a set of geometric solids.

Modeling the Activity

Review properties of the solid shapes. Choose a solid shape and ask: **Does this solid have any flat faces? How many?** Have the child describe other properties of the solid shape. Continue with other solid shapes.

Display the 3-Column Chart and tell the child he or she will sort the solids into three groups. Say: **Choose three labels from the pile. Place one at the top of each column.** Read the label in the first column. Say: **Look at the solid shapes. What solid shapes will you put in this column?**

Repeat sorting solid shapes into the remaining columns. Discuss why some shapes will go into more than one column. Then have the child clear the chart and choose three different labels to continue.

> **Helpful Hint**
>
> You may suggest that a child place a numbered, removable sticker on each face, edge, or corner as they count.

USE AFTER
LESSON 7.5

OBJECTIVE Identify and describe solid shapes using real-life solids

Face to Face
Variation

Before the Activity

Repeat "Face to Face" as described in Lesson 7.4. Vary the activity by having children use real-life solids. You may need to review real-life solids side by side with geometric solids.

Modeling the Activity

Hold up a real-life solid and ask: **How many faces does the [tissue box] have? Look at the geometric shapes. What shape has the same number of faces?** Then remind children they can count corners and edges to describe the solids. Have children place the geometric solid that matches the [tissue box] on the 3-Column Chart. Have children continue to find and sort objects in the classroom with the attributes of the solid shapes.

> **Helpful Hint**
>
> Have children count one attribute on a real-life solid and then on the geometric solid to see if it matches. Have them continue with other attributes to check.

Shape Art

CROSS-CURRICULAR
Art

OBJECTIVE Identify the
faces of solid shapes

MANAGEMENT Pairs

TIME 20 minutes

MATERIALS PER PAIR
- Shape Art (p. 159)

- pictures of Cubist
  paintings

- geometric solids

- tracing paper

- construction paper

- paste

- scissors

Before the Activity

Display pictures created during the Cubism period of art that
have identifiable plane or solid shapes. (Pablo Picasso and
George Braques were leaders in the Cubist era.) Place tracing
paper and a set of geometric solid shapes on the table.

Modeling the Activity

Focus childrens' attention on the pictures of Cubist paintings.
Explain that this style of painting got its name because
people thought some of the early paintings of this period
were made from little cubes. Choose one picture. Ask: **What
shapes do you see?** Have a volunteer use a piece of tracing
paper and trace around each shape as it is found. Tell
children that they will be creating their own piece of artwork
by tracing around the faces of solid shapes.

Have children look at the paper with the tracings. Point to
one shape and ask: **Which solid has a face that is this shape?**
Now pick up a [cube] and have a child describe it. Ask: **How
many faces does it have? What shape is each face?**
Demonstrate how to trace one face of the cube onto a sheet
of construction paper. Cut it out and place it aside. Repeat
with the other geometric shapes.

Have pairs take turns choosing solid shapes and tracing the
face onto construction paper. Then they cut out each plane
shape. Finally, pairs arrange and paste the shapes onto a
sheet of paper to make their own "Cubist" picture.

NUMBER OF THE WEEK
Spotlight on 4

NUMBER SENSE

OBJECTIVE Use the number 4 to solve problems in different contexts

MANAGEMENT Individuals

TIME 15 minutes

MATERIALS
- Spotlight on 4 (p. 210)
- geometric solid shapes set

Before the Activity

Make a copy of Spotlight on 4 (p. 210) for each child. Display a set of geometric solid shapes.

Modeling the Activity

Show children the Spotlight on 4 sheet. Say: **Today you will explore different ways to use the number 4.** Read the first activity. Have children look at the solid shapes and name each one. Then choose a solid shape [cube]. Have four volunteers find a different classroom item that has the same solid shape as the [cube].

Give each child a copy of Spotlight on 4. Read the other exercises to the class and answer any questions children may have before you continue. When all children have finished, review the answers with the class.

Answers

1. Children should draw a square or a rectangle.
2. Children should draw 2 sets of 4 circles each.
3. 4
4. Children should draw two diagonal lines, corner to corner.

Unit 3 Planner
Chapter 8

Use after . . .

LESSON 8.1
Put It There

For each pair:
- Put It There, p. 160
- Playing Card Master, p. 274
- counters

LESSON 8.2
Where Can It Be?

For each pair:
- Playing Card Master, p. 274
- magazine pages

LESSON 8.3
Who's Where?

For each pair:
- Neighborhood Gameboard, pp. 300–301
- counters

LESSON 8.4
Slides, Flips, and Turns

For each pair:
- Slides, Flips, and Turns, p. 161
- Playing Card Master, p. 274
- Geoboard Dot Paper, p. 237
- pattern blocks

LESSON 8.5
Patterns of the Past
Cross-Curricular

For each student:
- Patterns of the Past, p. 162
- Inch Grid Paper, p. 239
- connecting cubes (2 colors)
- crayons (2 colors)

LESSON 8.6
Keep It Going

For each group:
- pattern blocks

LESSON 8.7
Picture Parts
Cross-Curricular

For each student:
- Picture Parts, p. 163
- pictures of buildings
- 12-inch length of yarn

LESSON 8.8
Number of the Week Spotlight on 2

For each student:
- Spotlight on 2, p. 211

Chapter 8

USE AFTER LESSON 8.1

OBJECTIVE Follow directions about position and location of objects in space

MANAGEMENT Pairs

TIME 15 minutes

MATERIALS PER PAIR
- Put It There (p. 160)
- Playing Card Master (p. 274)
- counters

Put It There

Before the Activity

Make three copies of Playing Card Master (p. 274). Fill each space on one copy with the following words: *left, right, between, over,* and *under.* Repeat words randomly to fill all spaces. Cut out the cards and mix them up. Make a gameboard for each child. Label each gameboard with the same position words in random order. Each gameboard should be different.

Modeling the Activity

Display the gameboard. Place the cards facedown in a pile. Partners use different color counters.

Choose a volunteer to help you demonstrate the game. Point to the gameboard and say: **We will play a game using these position words.** Take a card from the top of the pile. Say: **My card says** *left.* **I put my game piece to the [left] of the card.** Demonstrate putting your game piece to the *left* of the card. Now have your partner find a word on their gameboard that matches the card. Say: **Place a counter on top of the word** *left.* If the child matches the word, then they switch roles. If the child does not match the word, then the partner has a turn to cover a space on his or her board.

Partners keep taking turns and placing game pieces in the correct places until one player covers three spaces in a row or column.

Helpful Hint

Tell children that they may use two counters placed on either side of the card to show *between.*

Where Can It Be?

OBJECTIVE Describe and locate the position, proximity, and direction of objects in the classroom

MANAGEMENT Pairs

TIME 15 minutes

MATERIALS PER PAIR
- Playing Card Master (p. 274)

- magazine pages

Before the Activity

Use the Playing Card Master (p. 274) to prepare vocabulary cards with position words: *behind, in front, far, near, next to, up, down, right,* and *left.* Cut apart the cards. Display pictures from magazines that depict the position words on the cards.

Modeling the Activity

Review the words on the cards with children. Have volunteers find the location of specific items in the magazine pages as you read each word aloud. For example, say: **What is behind [the dog?]** Then mix up the cards and place them facedown in a pile. Explain to the children that they will use the cards to identify the position of real-life objects in the classroom.

Have a volunteer help you demonstrate how to play.
Say: **Both partners choose an object in the classroom.**
Decide with your volunteer on an object, such as a table.
Now say: **Turn over the top card in the pile. Read the position word (*next to*).** Explain that each partner needs to find something in the classroom that is *next to* the table. Demonstrate by locating an object *next to* the table. Stand beside it and say: **The chair is *next to* the table.** Have your partner identify another object that is *next to* the table. The turn ends when partners agree that both objects show the position *next to*.

Children continue playing, finding objects to match the position on the card until all cards are used.

USE AFTER LESSON 8.3

OBJECTIVE Give and follow directions

MANAGEMENT Pairs

TIME 15 minutes

MATERIALS PER PAIR
- Neighborhood Gameboard (pp. 300–301)
- counters

Who's Where?

Before the Activity

Make a copy of the Neighborhood Gameboard (pp. 300–301) for each pair. Write the following on the board:

Josh is at the fire station.
He walks 2 spaces to the right.
Then he walks 6 spaces down.
Finally he walks 2 spaces left.
Where is Josh now?

Modeling the Activity

Display the gameboard. Have a volunteer help you demonstrate how to play. Say: **Place your counter on the space in front of the [store].** Then say position words and have him or her move the piece around the board. For example, say: **Move 3 spaces to the right. Move 5 spaces down.** Now read aloud the directions on the board. Tell children the counter will take the place of Josh. Tell pairs they are going to follow directions and move their counter around the board. Reread the first line and ask: **How do you know where to put the counter to show where Josh is?** Guide children to look at the key and find the picture next to the fire station. Say: **Place your counter on the square under the fire station.**

Reread the second line. Ask: **Do you move left or right?** Guide the child to move the counters 2 spaces to the right. Continue with the other directions. After all directions have been given and followed, ask: **Where is your counter now?** Remind children to use the key to help them identify that Josh is at the school.

Have children use the key and choose a beginning place and an ending place. Have them make up their own directions. Then pairs take turns sharing their walking directions aloud with the class.

(**Helpful Hint**)

Have children point to each space and count aloud as they move their counter so they do not lose track of the number of spaces.

USE AFTER LESSON 8.4

Slides, Flips, and Turns

VOCABULARY

OBJECTIVE Demonstrate slides, flips, and turns

MANAGEMENT Pairs

TIME 15 minutes

MATERIALS PER PAIR
- Slides, Flips, and Turns (p. 161)
- Playing Card Master (p. 274)
- Geoboard Dot Paper (p. 237)
- pattern blocks

Before the Activity

Copy and prepare Playing Card Master (p. 274) with three of each label: *slide, flip,* and *turn.* Cut apart the cards. Copy Geoboard Dot Paper (p. 237) for each child, and Slides, Flips, and Turns (p. 161) for each pair. Display pattern blocks.

Modeling the Activity

Show children the cards. Ask volunteers to draw on the board to demonstrate each of the words. Now mix the cards and place them facedown in a pile. Explain that children will work in pairs to play a game using pattern blocks and the vocabulary cards.

Ask a volunteer to help you demonstrate how to play. Have children position their Geoboard Dot Paper horizontally. Say: **Choose a pattern block. Place it on the first board of your dot paper.** Demonstrate how to align the pattern block on the last column of dots. Then say: **Now trace the pattern block.**

Explain that the partner will then choose a card and read it aloud. Turn over the top card and say: **The card says *flip.*** Demonstrate flipping the shape and aligning it on the next square of dots. Then say: **Now trace the shape that shows *a flip.*** Trace the shape. Have the child show how to make a slide and a turn using the same pattern block.

Children take turns choosing a pattern block and a card, and drawing the slide, flip, or turn.

USE AFTER LESSON 8.5

Patterns of the Past

CROSS-CURRICULAR
Social Studies

OBJECTIVE Describe, predict, and extend a pattern

MANAGEMENT Individuals

TIME 15 minutes

MATERIALS
- Patterns of the Past (p. 162)
- Inch Grid Paper (p. 239)
- connecting cubes (2 colors)
- crayons (2 colors)

Before the Activity

Copy a sheet of Inch Grid Paper (p. 239) for each child. Display the Patterns of the Past (p. 162). Have children discuss what they know about quilts. Point out that quilts have patterns of shapes in them. Ask volunteers to identify the shapes and the patterns they see in the quilt on the activity sheet.

Modeling the Activity

Tell children they will use the Patterns of the Past to work with extending shape patterns. Point to the quilt pattern and have a volunteer say the pattern aloud. Ask: **How many colors do you see in the quilt?** Have the child gather that number of colors or cubes. Say: **Use the cubes to show the pattern in the first row of the quilt.** Demonstrate how to put the cubes together to model the pattern.

Then focus attention on the Inch Grid Paper and say: **Now you are going to copy the pattern on your grid paper. Choose two colors.** Demonstrate how to copy the pattern using crayons of two different colors.

Have children continue by copying the patterns and extending them in *Try This!*

(**Helpful Hint**)

Remind children that it might help them to recognize a pattern if they say the pattern aloud.

USE AFTER LESSON 8.6

OBJECTIVES Identify the pattern unit; extend patterns of shapes, colors, and numbers

MANAGEMENT Groups

TIME 15 minutes

MATERIALS PER GROUP
• pattern blocks

Keep It Going

Before the Activity

Display pattern blocks. Arrange the blocks into a pattern.

Modeling the Activity

Focus attention on the pattern blocks. Ask a volunteer to say the pattern aloud. Explain to children that they will play a pattern game using pattern blocks. Ask a volunteer to help you demonstrate the game. Say: **I will place six blocks on the table.** Arrange the blocks so they form a repeating pattern. For example: ABBABB. Ask: **What is the pattern?** Discuss the pattern with children.

Explain that your partner will add pattern blocks to continue the same pattern. Say: **Continue the pattern. Place two more pattern units to the end of the pattern.** Remind children that the pattern unit is the group of shapes that repeats and not just the last shape. Then have another volunteer continue the pattern.

Have children play in small groups. Play until each child has a chance to create the beginning pattern and have a classmate extend it.

Grade 1 • Chapter 8   59

Picture Parts

CROSS-CURRICULAR Art

OBJECTIVE Determine and draw symmetrical designs

MANAGEMENT Pairs

TIME 15 minutes

MATERIALS PER PAIR
- Picture Parts (p. 163)
- pictures of buildings
- 12-inch length of yarn
- tracing paper

Before the Activity

Display pictures of buildings that have symmetry. Make a copy of Picture Parts (p. 163) for each pair.

Modeling the Activity

Have children look at the buildings. Discuss the architecture. Tell how plans have to be drawn on paper before any building is built. Say: **You and a partner will draw plans for a symmetrical building.** Use a piece of tracing paper. With a dark marker, trace around one of the buildings. Ask: **How do you know this building is symmetrical?** Demonstrate how to fold the tracing down the middle. Then use a piece of yarn as the line of symmetry. Say: **Look at both sides of the building. Are they the same?** Encourage children to choose a building. Repeat the steps as you watch.

Now take a blank piece of tracing paper. Fold it in half. Open it and say: **I will draw the plan for half of a building on one side of the line.** Fold the paper again. Have a volunteer copy the outline on the other side of the paper. Open the paper and say: **Look at the building. Does it have symmetry?** Point to the line of symmetry. Point to the symmetry in each side.

Have children draw symmetrical details on their building.

USE AFTER LESSON 8.8

NUMBER OF THE WEEK
Spotlight on 2

NUMBER SENSE

OBJECTIVE Use the number 2 in different contexts

MANAGEMENT Individuals

TIME 20 minutes

MATERIALS
• Spotlight on 2 (p. 211)

Before the Activity

Make copies of Spotlight on 2 (p. 211) for each child.

Modeling the Activity

Show children the Spotlight on 2 sheet. Say: **You will be exploring different ways to use the number 2.** Read over the five problems and answer any questions children may have.

Give each child a copy of Spotlight on 2. When all children have finished, review the answers with the class.

Answers

1. Child draws 2 hearts over the star and 2 circles to the left.

2. 2 baskets

3. 2 bows

4. Child draws a dotted square and a flower square.

Unit 3 Planner
Chapter 9

Use after . . .

LESSON 9.1
Slice It Up

For each pair:
- Slice It Up, p. 164
- Geoboard Dot Paper, p. 237

LESSON 9.2
It's a Puzzle

For each pair:
- It's a Puzzle, p. 165
- Fractions $\frac{1}{2}$, $\frac{1}{3}$, $\frac{1}{4}$, p. 236
- small bags

LESSON 9.3
Follow Me

For each pair:
- Follow Me, p. 166
- Fractions $\frac{1}{2}$, $\frac{1}{3}$, $\frac{1}{4}$, p. 236
- crayons

LESSON 9.4
Rolling Fractions

For each student:
- number cube
- counters
- colored objects

LESSON 9.5
Cube Grab

For each group:
- Cube Grab, p. 167
- Bar Graph (3-Row), p. 232
- connecting cubes (6 green, 2 blue, 1 red)
- paper bag
- crayons (green, blue, and red)

LESSON 9.6
Number of the Week Spotlight on $\frac{1}{2}$

For each student:
- Spotlight on $\frac{1}{2}$, p. 212
- crayon

Chapter 9

USE AFTER LESSON 9.1

OBJECTIVE Identify and show equal parts in a plane figure

MANAGEMENT Pairs

TIME 15 minutes

MATERIALS PER PAIR
- Slice It Up (p. 164)
- Geoboard Dot Paper (p. 237)

Slice It Up

Before the Activity

Prepare and display rectangles of the same size that show one whole part, two equal parts, three equal parts, and four equal parts. Make a copy of the Geoboard Dot Paper (p. 237) for each child.

Modeling the Activity

Focus attention on the folded rectangles. Say: **Each rectangle has been folded into** *equal* **parts.** Have a volunteer tell how many equal parts each rectangle has. Remind children that equal parts are always the same size. Demonstrate drawing a square on your Geoboard Dot Paper. Ask: **How can you show equal parts?** Have a volunteer draw a line to show two equal parts on the square.

Now say: **Is there another way to show two equal parts on the square?** Allow children to draw the square on their page and draw different ways of showing two equal parts. Have pairs take turns drawing a shape and showing equal parts. Encourage them to show two, three, and four equal parts.

(**Helpful Hint**)

You may want to supply children with various cutout shapes so they can actually fold the shape into equal parts before drawing the line on their Geoboard Dot Paper.

It's a Puzzle

VOCABULARY

OBJECTIVE Identify one half of a whole

MANAGEMENT Pairs

TIME 15 minutes

MATERIALS PER PAIR
- It's a Puzzle (p. 165)
- Fractions $\frac{1}{2}$, $\frac{1}{3}$, $\frac{1}{4}$ (p. 236)
- small bags

Before the Activity

Make two copies of Fractions $\frac{1}{2}$, $\frac{1}{3}$, $\frac{1}{4}$ (p. 236) for each pair. Cut the shapes in the top row into halves. Place the two parts for each shape in a different paper bag. Save the shapes for thirds and fourths to use with other activities.

Modeling the Activity

Hold up a paper bag and explain that it contains puzzle parts to make a shape. Allow children to examine the parts in each bag. Say: **How many equal parts are in each bag?** Have a volunteer take both parts from a bag. Ask: **Can you put the parts together to make a whole? How many equal parts make a whole [shape]?** Now have the child hold up one part and ask: **What fraction of the [shape] are you holding up?** Write $\frac{1}{2}$ on the board.

Then ask: **What fraction of the [shape] is left if you place one part back in the bag?**

Have partners take turns pulling halves and writing $\frac{1}{2}$.

Helpful Hint

You can copy Fractions $\frac{1}{2}$, $\frac{1}{3}$, $\frac{1}{4}$ onto colored paper and then laminate it for durability before cutting the shapes.

Follow Me

VOCABULARY

OBJECTIVES Review parts of a whole; identify $\frac{1}{2}$, $\frac{1}{3}$, and $\frac{1}{4}$

MANAGEMENT Pairs

TIME 15 minutes

MATERIALS PER PAIR
- Follow Me (p. 166)
- Fractions $\frac{1}{2}$, $\frac{1}{3}$, $\frac{1}{4}$ (p. 236)
- crayons

Before the Activity

Copy a Fractions $\frac{1}{2}$, $\frac{1}{3}$, $\frac{1}{4}$ sheet (p. 236) for each child. Display the Follow Me sheet (p. 166).

Modeling the Activity

Focus attention on the Fractions $\frac{1}{2}$, $\frac{1}{3}$, $\frac{1}{4}$ sheet. Demonstrate playing the Follow Me game with a volunteer. Say: **Look at the first shape. I am going to color part of the square.** Have your partner cover his or her eyes. Color one half of the square orange. Say: **Uncover your eyes. Color one half of your square orange.** Remind children the 1 in $\frac{1}{2}$ represents 1 part of 2, so they color only 1 of the 2 parts to show $\frac{1}{2}$. The same rule applies for $\frac{1}{3}$ and $\frac{1}{4}$.

Now hold up both sheets. Say: **Look at both squares. Do both squares have equal parts colored orange?** Allow time for discussion.

Tell partners to take turns giving and following directions until they have colored each shape. Tell children to use the words *one half, one third,* and *one fourth* in their directions.

Rolling Fractions

USE AFTER LESSON 9.4

OBJECTIVES Identify fractions for part of a set; understand the meaning of the numbers in a fraction

MANAGEMENT Individuals

TIME 20 minutes

MATERIALS
- number cube
- counters
- colored objects

Before the Activity

Label the number cube with numbers 2, 2, 2, 3, 3, 3.

Modeling the Activity

Tell children they will find different parts of a set. Roll the number cube. Say: **What number does it show? [3]** Place that number of red counters on the table. Place one yellow counter in the set.

Find what fraction names the number of yellow counters. Ask: **How many counters are in the set?** Tell children this is the bottom number in the fraction. Ask: **How many counters are yellow? This is the top number in the fraction.** Have a volunteer write the fraction. Remind children that $\frac{1}{4}$ stands for 1 [yellow] part of 4 parts.

Next, have children demonstrate the fraction using real-life objects in the set. For example, children can group three red crayons and one yellow crayon to show $\frac{1}{4}$. Encourage children to describe their set and then name the fraction. Continue the number cube activity and demonstrating the fractions with sets of real-life objects.

Cube Grab

USE AFTER LESSON 9.5

OBJECTIVE Predict and determine the probability of an event

MANAGEMENT Groups

TIME 15 minutes

MATERIALS PER GROUP
- Cube Grab (p. 167)
- 3-Row Bar Graph (p. 232)
- connecting cubes (6 green, 2 blue, 1 red)
- paper bag
- crayons (green, blue, red)

Before the Activity

Discuss real-life events that are certain, impossible, or probable. Prepare a 3-Row Bar Graph (p. 232) with a title and the following labels: *Green, Red,* and *Blue.* Draw a corresponding color cube above each label. Group the connecting cubes by color.

Modeling the Activity

Focus attention on the Bar Graph Form and the connecting cubes. Discuss what it means to make a prediction. Then say: **Look at the groups of cubes. Describe each group.** Encourage children to see that there are many more green cubes. Place the cubes in the bag and have a volunteer help you demonstrate. Explain that he or she will pull a cube from the bag and then color a box on the graph. Before you begin, ask the child: **What color will you *most likely* pick? Why?** Discuss the response. Have the child pick a cube and record it on the graph. Then return the cube to the bag.

Continue the activity by having children tell which color they predict they will most likely or least likely pick and why. Discuss childrens' predictions and the results. Color in the graph until one row is full.

USE AFTER LESSON 9.6

NUMBER OF THE WEEK
Spotlight on $\frac{1}{2}$

NUMBER SENSE

OBJECTIVE Use the number $\frac{1}{2}$ to solve problems in many contexts

MANAGEMENT Individuals

TIME 15 minutes

MATERIALS
- Spotlight on $\frac{1}{2}$ (p. 212)
- crayon

Before the Activity

Make a copy of Spotlight on $\frac{1}{2}$ (p. 212) for each child.

Modeling the Activity

Show children the Spotlight on $\frac{1}{2}$ sheet. Say: **Today we will explore different ways to use the fraction $\frac{1}{2}$.** Read the first activity and ask: **How many equal parts does the diamond have? Color $\frac{1}{2}$.** Hold up the sheet and review what each number represents in the fraction $\frac{1}{2}$.

Give each child a copy of Spotlight on $\frac{1}{2}$. Read the other exercises to the class and answer any questions children may have before you continue. When all children have finished, review the answers with the class.

Answers

1. Children should color $\frac{1}{2}$ of the diamond.

2. Children should color 2 marbles.

3. Children should draw a square and color $\frac{1}{2}$.

4. *Answers may vary. Sample:* I drew a set and circled one half of it.

Unit 4 Planner
Chapter 10

Use after . . .

LESSON 10.1
Count By Groups

For each group:
- Playing Card Master, p. 274
- 450 paper clips
- 9 plastic bags

LESSON 10.2
Spin and Count

For each pair:
- Spin and Count, p. 168
- 3-Column Chart, p. 227
- 10-Part Spinner, p. 280
- connecting cubes (10 red, 9 blue)

LESSON 10.3
Show Your Number

For each pair:
- Number Cards 20–50, pp. 264–267
- 2-Column Chart, p. 226
- tens and ones blocks

LESSON 10.4
Show Your Number *Variation*

For each pair:
- Number Cards 20–50, pp. 264–267
- 2-Column Chart, p. 226
- tens and ones blocks

LESSON 10.5
Number Switch

For each pair:
- Number Switch, p. 169
- 2-Column Chart, p. 226
- Number Cards 0–9, pp. 262–263
- 9 tens blocks and 9 ones blocks

LESSON 10.6
Roll and Write

For each pair:
- Roll and Write, p. 170
- 2-Column Chart, p. 226
- 2 number cubes
- 6 tens blocks and 9 ones blocks

LESSON 10.7
Pick a Number

For each pair:
- Pick a Number, p. 171
- Hundred Chart, p. 238
- tens and ones blocks
- crayons
- paper bag

LESSON 10.8
Number of the Week Spotlight on 10

For each student:
- Spotlight on 10 p. 213
- crayon

Chapter 10

OBJECTIVES Make groups of 10; write and read decade names to 90

MANAGEMENT Groups

TIME 15 minutes

MATERIALS PER GROUP
- Playing Card Master (p. 274)
- 450 paper clips
- 9 plastic bags

Count by Groups

Before the Activity

Fill nine plastic bags with paper clips. Each should contain from 10 to 90 paper clips in multiples of ten. Also prepare two Playing Card Masters (p. 274), one with the numbers *10, 20, 30, 40, 50, 60, 70, 80, 90,* and one with the corresponding number words *ten* to *ninety*.

Modeling the Activity

Say: **When you count objects, sometimes it's easier to count by tens.** Display a bag of 20 paper clips. Remove the paper clips and say: **I want to build groups of ten. Let's count ten together.** Hold up each paper clip as children count with you. Make a train of ten paper clips. Display it and say: **Now I've made one group of ten. Let's see if I have enough paper clips left to make another group of ten. Let's count together.** Display the remaining paper clips as children count with you. Say: **Yes, I can make another group of ten.** Make a second ten train and display it.

Display both trains. Ask: **How many groups of ten do I have? How many paper clips do I have in all?** Ask a volunteer to find the card that has the number *20* and the number word *twenty.* Display the cards and say: **These cards show the number of paper clips in this bag.**

Have a volunteer repeat the process. Then say: **When we've matched all the number cards and word cards with the bags, we'll put them in order from the least number to the greatest number.**

> **Helpful Hint**

Make sure children understand they are to build groups of ten only, not groups of any other number.

USE AFTER LESSON 10.2

Spin and Count

OBJECTIVES Count and write how many tens and ones; read and write the numerals 10 through 19

MANAGEMENT Pairs

TIME 15 minutes

MATERIALS PER PAIR
- Spin and Count (p. 168)
- 3-Column Chart (p. 227)
- Blank Spinner (p. 276)
- 10 red and 9 blue connecting cubes

Before the Activity

At the top of the 3-Column Chart (p. 227), print *tens* above the left column, *ones* above the middle column, and *number* above the right column. Copy for children's use. Use the Blank Spinner and draw 10 equal sections on it. Number them 0 through 9.

Modeling the Activity

Begin by building a ten-cube train with the red connecting cubes. Have a volunteer count them. Say: **This is a ten.** Next, spin the spinner. Have a volunteer identify the number. Count out that many blue connecting cubes. Say: **These are ones.** Have a volunteer count the blue connecting cubes.

Point to the appropriate boxes on the 3-Column Chart and say: **In this column, I'll write how many tens there are.** Write *1* in the tens column. **In this column, I'll write how many ones there are.** Write that number in the ones column. **How many cubes are there in all? I'll write that number in this column.** Write that number in the right column.

Helpful Hint

Make sure that children count the ten-cube train as ten, not as one, when they are counting.

USE AFTER
LESSON 10.3

Show Your Number

VOCABULARY

OBJECTIVE Read and model numbers to 50 and identify tens and ones

MANAGEMENT Pairs

TIME 15 minutes

MATERIALS PER PAIR
- Number Cards 20–50 (pp. 264–267)
- 2-Column Chart (p. 226)
- tens and ones blocks

Before the Activity

Select the cards numbered 20 to 50 from the Number Cards (pp. 264–267). Copy a 2-Column Chart (p. 226). Label the columns *tens* and *ones* and review the words with children.

Modeling the Activity

Ask a volunteer to play a game with you. Say: **We're going to play a card game.** Mix the cards up and place them facedown on a table. Say: **Now my partner will turn over the top card so we can both see the number.**

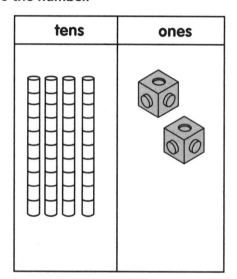

Ask: **What is the number?** The volunteer reads the number aloud, for example 42. Then say: **Now you will show the number on your 2-Column Chart.** Guide the volunteer in placing four tens blocks and two ones blocks on the chart. Say: **Now I will check the number to make sure there are the correct amount of tens and ones blocks.**

Tell children to continue to play until all cards have been picked.

USE AFTER LESSON 10.4

Show Your Number
Variation

Before the Activity

Label the columns on the 2-Column Chart (p. 226) as *tens* and *ones.*

Modeling the Activity

Repeat "Show Your Number," as described in Lesson 10.3 (p. 70). Vary the activity by using the Number Cards 51 to 90.

VOCABULARY

OBJECTIVES Read and model numbers for 51 to 90; identify tens and ones

---

USE AFTER LESSON 10.5

Number Switch

Before the Activity

Select cards zero to nine from two Number Card decks. Prepare the 2-Column Chart (p. 226), by writing *tens* and *ones* in the appropriate columns.

Modeling the Activity

Mix each set of Number Cards separately and place them facedown in two piles. Ask a volunteer to turn over a card from each pile. Say, for example: **My partner has turned over two and four. I know a number that we can make with them.** Place the cards side by side and display 24. Say: **I have made 24. I can show 24 another way.** Place two tens blocks in the *tens* column on the 2-Column Chart and four ones blocks in the *ones* column. Say: **These tens blocks are in the tens column. These ones blocks are in the ones column. Together, they show 24.**

Then ask: **Can anyone think of a new number that my partner and I can make by switching the cards?** After children respond, say: **By switching our cards, we can make 42.** Reverse the cards to show how 24 changes to 42. Say: **I can show 42 another way too.** Take four tens blocks and two ones blocks and place them in the appropriate columns on the 2-Column Chart. Ask: **How many are in the tens column? How many are in the ones column? What number do they show?** Keep trying it, two cards at a time.

OBJECTIVE Write how many tens and ones

MANAGEMENT Pairs

TIME 15 minutes

MATERIALS PER PAIR
- Number Switch (p. 169)
- 2-Column Chart (p. 226)
- Number Cards (pp. 262–263)
- 9 tens blocks, 9 ones blocks

Teacher Notes

Roll and Write

OBJECTIVE Use place-value blocks and expanded notation to represent 2-digit numbers

MANAGEMENT Pairs

TIME 15 minutes

MATERIALS PER PAIR
- Roll and Write (p. 170)
- 2-Column Chart (p. 226)
- 2 Number Cubes
- 6 tens blocks and 9 ones blocks

Before the Activity

Label one Number Cube 1–6 and the other Number Cube 4–9. Prepare the 2-Column Chart (p. 226), by writing *tens* and *ones* in the appropriate columns.

Modeling the Activity

Say: **Most grown-ups use 2-digit numbers to tell their age. This activity is about 2-digit numbers.** Ask a volunteer to roll first one cube and then the other. Say, for example: **My partner has rolled a three and six. I know a number that we can make with them.** Place the cubes side by side and display 36. Say: **I have made 36. I can show 36 another way.** Place the blocks in the appropriate columns on the 2-Column Chart. Say: **The three tens blocks are in the tens column. The six ones blocks are in the ones column. Together, they show 36.**

Then ask: **Can anyone think of another way to write the number?** After children respond, say: **Yes, you can write the number using an addition sign.** Demonstrate by writing 30 + 6 = 36 on the board.

Pick a Number

VOCABULARY

OBJECTIVE Identify numbers through 100

MANAGEMENT Pairs

TIME 15 minutes

MATERIALS PER PAIR
- Pick a Number (p. 171)
- Hundred Chart (p. 238)
- tens and ones blocks
- crayons
- paper bag

Before the Activity

Make one copy of the Hundred Chart (p. 238) for each pair of children. Prepare a bag filled with tens and ones blocks.

Modeling the Activity

Begin by displaying the Hundred Chart and the pile of squares. Say: **This is a Hundred Chart. It shows the numbers from 1 to 100. In the bag there are tens and ones blocks.** Call on a volunteer to pick a handful of blocks from the bag. Say: **How many different numbers can you show with these blocks?** Begin with 1 ones block. Say: **You can show the number 1 with the ones block.** Then have the volunteer record the number 1 by coloring in the number on the Hundred Chart. Demonstrate how they can show and record other numbers with the handful of blocks.

After children form pairs, give each pair a Hundred Chart. Then have each child take a handful of blocks from the bag and begin the activity. Say: **Use the blocks to make as many different numbers as you can.**

> **Helpful Hint**
>
> Remind partners to combine the blocks they picked to show greater numbers.

USE AFTER LESSON 10.8

NUMBER OF THE WEEK
Spotlight on 10

NUMBER SENSE

OBJECTIVE Use the number 10 to solve problems in many contexts

MANAGEMENT Individuals

TIME 15 minutes

MATERIALS
- Spotlight on 10 (p. 213)
- crayon

Before the Activity

Make a copy of Spotlight on 10 (p. 213) for each child.

Modeling the Activity

Show children the Spotlight on 10 sheet. Say: **Today we will explore different ways to use 10.** Read the first activity and ask: **What number is the whole? What numbers are the parts?** Hold up the sheet and point to the numbers. Say: **You are going to make the fact family using 10, 8, and 2.**

Give each child a copy of Spotlight on 10. Read the other exercises to the class and answer any questions children may have before you continue. When all children have finished, review the answers with the class.

Answers

1. $8 + 2 = 10$; $2 + 8 = 10$; $10 - 8 = 2$; $10 - 2 = 8$
2. 10
3. Children should color 5 buttons.
4. Children should draw a horizontal line through the center of the 10.

Unit 4 Planner
Chapter 11

Use after . . .

LESSON 11.1
Before and After Move It!

For each pair:
- 3-Column Chart, p. 227
- Move It! Gameboard, pp. 298–299
- Hundred Chart, p. 238
- 16 two-sided counters
- envelope

LESSON 11.2
Number Lineup

For each pair:
- Number Lineup, p. 172
- Playing Card Master, p. 274 (2 copies)
- construction paper
- counter

LESSON 11.3
Best Guess
Cross-Curricular

For each group:
- Best Guess, p. 173
- pictures of large groups of animals
- paper clips
- small bowl

LESSON 11.4
Compare Your Numbers

For each pair:
- Number Cards 0–100, pp. 262–273

LESSON 11.5
Compare Your Numbers
Variation

For each pair:
- Number Cards 0–100, pp. 262–273

LESSON 11.6
Number of the Week Spotlight on 99

For each student:
- Spotlight on 99, p. 214

Chapter 11

**USE AFTER
LESSON 11.1**

OBJECTIVE Find the number that comes before, between, or after

MANAGEMENT Pairs

TIME 20 minutes

MATERIALS PER PAIR
- 3-Column Chart (p. 227)
- Move It! Gameboard (pp. 298–299)
- Hundred Chart (p. 238)
- 16 two-sided counters
- envelope

Before and After Move It!

Before the Activity

Prepare 3-Column Chart (p. 227) with labels: *Before, Number, After.* Cut apart the Hundred Chart (p. 238). Place the numbers in an envelope. Display the Move It! Gameboard (pp. 298–299).

Modeling the Activity

Ask a volunteer to help you demonstrate. Show how to set up the gameboard. Say: **Each partner will choose a color counter. Place 8 counters on the gameboard.**

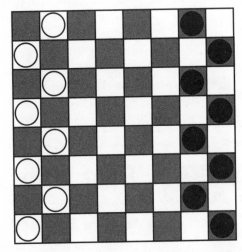

Choose a number from the envelope. Point to the chart and say: **I will write the number in the column labeled *Number.*** Instruct your partner to find the number *before* or *after.* Say: **Find the number *before.* Write the number on the chart.** Direct the child to the correct column on the chart. Remind children they can put numbers on a number line to help them find a number that comes before or after. When the correct answer is found say: **Move one of your counters forward on the gameboard.**

Partners will switch roles and repeat the activity. The game ends when one player moves all of his or her counters to the other side of the gameboard.

Helpful Hint

You may need to explain the basic moves in the traditional game of checkers, if children are not familiar with them. Tell children that checkers is a game that people have been playing for more than 150 years.

Number Lineup

VOCABULARY

OBJECTIVE Identify ordinal positions *first* through *tenth*

MANAGEMENT Pairs

TIME 15 minutes

MATERIALS PER PAIR
- Number Lineup (p. 172)
- Playing Card Master (p. 274) (2 copies)
- construction paper
- counter

Before the Activity

Display Number Lineup (p. 172). Cut out ten squares from construction paper. Use the Playing Card Master (p. 274) to make ten vocabulary cards with the ordinal numbers *first* through *tenth*.

Modeling the Activity

Place the ten construction paper squares in a row. Have a child put a counter on a square. Ask: **What position in line is the square you picked? [fourth]** Point to each square as children count. Say: **First, second, third, [fourth]. The card picked is the [fourth] card in the row.** Remind children that they can count the cardinal numbers to emphasize the order before counting the ordinal numbers.

Have another child find the card that has the word [fourth] written on it. Say: **Now place the card under the [fourth] square.** Partners take turns placing a counter on a square and finding the word card that tells where the counter is placed. Emphasize that while placing the word card on the square the child should say the ordinal number.

Best Guess

CROSS-CURRICULAR Science

OBJECTIVE Estimate how many are in a group, using 10 as a referent

MANAGEMENT Groups

TIME 15 minutes

MATERIALS PER GROUP
- Best Guess (p. 173)
- pictures of large groups of animals
- paper clips
- small bowl

Before the Activity

Display pictures of animals that travel in large groups and a copy of Best Guess (p. 173). Place 20–100 paper clips in a bowl for each group.

Modeling the Activity

Direct attention to the animal pictures. Point out how some animals travel in very large groups. Discuss how scientists often have to estimate when counting animals in such large groups. Now show children the bowl with paper clips and tell them they will estimate how many paper clips in all. Remind children that an estimate is a good guess and not an exact amount. Count out ten paper clips. Ask: **How can you use the group of ten to help you estimate?**

Pour the remaining paper clips in the bowl onto the table. Say: **Look at what a group of ten paper clips looks like. Use this to estimate how many tens are in the larger group.** Say: **Now estimate how many paper clips in all.** Remind children to include the group of ten when estimating how many in all. Write responses on the board. Say: **Count on from ten to find the exact amount.** Count on with children. Write the exact number on the board and compare it to the estimates. Groups repeat the activity beginning with a different number of paper clips.

USE AFTER LESSON 11.4

VOCABULARY

OBJECTIVE Compare two numbers using the terms *greater than* or *less than*

MANAGEMENT Pairs

TIME 15 minutes

MATERIALS PER PAIR
- Number Cards 0–50 (pp. 262–267)
- Number Cards 51–100 (pp. 268–273)

Compare Your Numbers

Before the Activity

Prepare Number Cards 0–50 (pp. 262–267) and 51–100 (pp. 268–273). Make two piles of twenty cards between 20 and 99.

Modeling the Activity

Ask two volunteers to demonstrate the game "Compare Your Numbers." Place a pile of cards in front of each child. Say: **Mix the cards. Then place them facedown on the table.** Explain that each child will turn over the top card. Then they will decide which number is greater or which number is less. Say: **Turn over the top card. Say your number aloud.** Then ask: **Which number is greater?** Remind children they can cover the ones in each number and focus on the tens to help them compare.

Partners continue playing. The player who has the greater number keeps both cards. The player that has the number that is less begins the next round by asking: **Is my number greater or less than your number?** Play until all cards are used.

Compare Your Numbers
Variation

OBJECTIVE Compare two numbers using > or <

MANAGEMENT Pairs

TIME 15 minutes

MATERIALS PER PAIR
- Number Cards 0–50 (pp. 262–267)
- Number Cards 51–100 (pp. 268–273)
- index cards

Before the Activity

Repeat "Compare Your Numbers" as described in Lesson 11.4. Vary the activity by using the symbols for greater than (>) and less than (<). Use Number Cards 0–50 (pp. 262–267) and Number Cards 51–100 (pp. 268–273) to prepare two piles of twenty cards between 20 and 99. Prepare an index card for each child by writing the symbols > and < on the cards.

Modeling the Activity

Play "Compare Your Numbers," following the directions on page 77. Play the same activity, but have children place their Number Cards on the table side by side. Then they use their symbol card (>) or (<) to compare. If the numbers are equal, they each keep their Number Card.

NUMBER OF THE WEEK
Spotlight on 99

NUMBER SENSE

OBJECTIVE Use the number 99 to solve problems in many contexts

MANAGEMENT Individuals

TIME 15 minutes

MATERIALS
- Spotlight on 99 (p. 214)

Before the Activity

Make a copy of Spotlight on 99 (p. 214) for each child.

Modeling the Activity

Show children the Spotlight on 99 sheet. Say: **Today we will explore different ways you can use the number 99.** Read the first activity and ask: **Which number is greater?** Have a volunteer draw the symbol that shows *greater than* or *less than.* Remind children that the arrow always points to the lesser number and opens to the greater number.

Give each child a copy of Spotlight on 99. Read the other exercises to the class. After each set of directions, give children time to complete the exercise before moving on to the next set of directions.

Answers

1. 99 > 96

2. 100

3. about 9 marbles

4. Children circle 10 tally marks; *Estimates will vary;* 99

Unit 4 Planner
Chapter 12

Use after . . .

LESSON 12.1
Count by Groups
Variation

For each group:
- Playing Card Master, p. 274
- 45 paper clips
- 9 plastic bags

LESSON 12.2
Missing Links
Cross-Curricular

For each pair:
- Missing Links, p. 174
- index cards
- items in nature with sets of 5
- paper clips

LESSON 12.3
What's My Seat Number?

For each pair:
- What's My Seat Number?, p. 175
- Hundred Chart, p. 238
- Number Cards 10–40, pp. 263–266
- index cards

LESSON 12.4
Odd or Even?
Vocabulary

For each pair:
- Odd or Even?, p. 176
- 2-Column Chart, p. 226
- Number Cards 1–20, pp. 262–264
- 20 connecting cubes

LESSON 12.5
Number of the Week
Spotlight on 50

For each student:
- Spotlight on 50, p. 215

Chapter 12

USE AFTER LESSON 12.1

OBJECTIVE Count by 2s

Count by Groups
Variation

Before the Activity

Repeat "Count by Groups," as described in Lesson 10.1. Vary the activity by counting groups by 2s. Use bags with an even number of 2 to 20 cubes. Children can write the numbers to show how they count.

Modeling the Activity

Play "Count by Groups," following the directions on page 68. Play the same activity, but have children count by 2s and then write the numbers.

USE AFTER LESSON 12.2

CROSS-CURRICULAR Science

OBJECTIVE Count by 5s to 100

MANAGEMENT Pairs

TIME 15 minutes

MATERIALS PER PAIR
• Missing Links (p. 174)
• index cards
• item in nature with sets of 5
• paper clips

Missing Links

Before the Activity

Make index cards for multiples of 5 from 5–100 for each pair. Display things in nature that show 5. For example, cut a cross section of a pear or apple; or find a picture of a starfish. Ask children for ideas of things in nature that they can think of that come in sets of 5. Record each idea.

Modeling the Activity

Choose a volunteer to help you demonstrate sets of 5. Count out 45 paper clips as children count aloud. Say: **Make strings of 5 clips each.** Allow two more volunteers to help string the clips. Then say: **Line up the strings of 5 paper clips. Count by 5s to find how many in all.** Then say: **Now put a number card under each string of paper clips.** Have the class count aloud by 5s as the child places the number cards in order under each string of paper clips.

Next, have your partner close his or her eyes. Say: **I will take away a number card.** Remove a card. Have your partner open his or her eyes. Ask: **How can you find what number is missing?** Encourage the child to count aloud from 5 as he or she finds the missing number. Allow time for each child to skip count and remove a card.

What's My Seat Number?

OBJECTIVES Identify
1 more, 1 less, 10 more,
10 less

MANAGEMENT Pairs

TIME 15 minutes

MATERIALS PER PAIR
- What's My Seat Number?
  (p. 175)

- Hundred Chart (p. 238)

- Number Cards 10–40
  (pp. 263–266)

- index cards

Before the Activity

Ask children if they have ever been to a theater. Tell them
that each ticket has a matching seat number. Copy the top
half of the Hundred Chart (p. 238) for children's use. Copy
and separate out Number Cards 10–40 (pp. 263–266). Write
one of the following terms on each of four index cards:
1 more, 1 less, 10 more, 10 less.

Modeling the Activity

Mix the Number Cards and place them facedown on the
table. Mix the word cards and place them facedown on the
table. Show children the hundred chart and tell them to
imagine that these are the seats in a theater.

Choose a volunteer to help you demonstrate. Say: **We are
going to find our seats by using word clues.** Have your
partner focus on the two card piles. Say: **Choose the top card
from each pile. What number did you choose?** [32] **Now read
the clue card.** Help the child read the words on the card.
[10 more] Tell the child that the number and the clue card
will help him or her find the correct seat on the hundred
chart. For example say: **Your seat number is [10 more] than
[32]. What is your seat number?** After they respond,
say: **[10 more] than [32] is [42]. Your seat number is [42].**

Guide children in finding and coloring in [42] on the hundred
chart. Place the clue card back in the pile. Partners take turns
picking cards from each pile and using the clues to find each
other's seat numbers.

Odd or Even?

VOCABULARY

OBJECTIVE Discover odd and even numbers

MANAGEMENT Pairs

TIME 15 minutes

MATERIALS PER PAIR

- Odd or Even? (p. 176)

- 2-Column Chart (p. 226)

- Number Cards 1–20 (pp. 262–264)

- 20 cubes

Before the Activity

Prepare a 2-Column Chart (p. 226) with the following heads: *odd* in the left column and *even* in the right column. Make a copy for each pair. Copy Number Cards 1–20 (pp. 262–264).

Modeling the Activity

Display the cards facedown in a pile along with the cubes. Tell children they will use the cubes to identify odd and even numbers. Have a volunteer help you demonstrate. Say: **Pick a Number Card. Read the number aloud.** [7]. Guide the child to count out that many cubes. Say: **Now I will place the cubes in pairs.** Display the pairs and ask: **How do the pairs help me show odd or even?** Remind children that if there is a leftover cube, the number is odd. **Is the number** [7] **odd or even?** Write the number [7] in the *odd* column of the chart.

Pairs take turns. One partner chooses a number and reads it aloud. The other partner makes cube pairs and writes the number on the chart. Continue until each child has written 5 numbers.

NUMBER OF THE WEEK
Spotlight on 50

NUMBER SENSE

OBJECTIVE Use the number 50 to solve problems in many contexts

MANAGEMENT Individuals

TIME 15 minutes

MATERIALS

- Spotlight on 50 (p. 215)

Before the Activity

Make a copy of Spotlight on 50 (p. 215) for each child.

Modeling the Activity

Show children the Spotlight on 50 sheet. Say: **Today we will explore different ways you can use the number 50.** Read the first activity and have a volunteer count by fives to 50. Ask: **How many petals are there in all?**

Ask a volunteer to read the other activities to the class. After each set of directions, give children time to complete the exercise before moving on to the next set of directions.

Answers

1. 50

2. Child draws 10 tally marks; 50 stamps.

3. Child circles the square with 30.

4. less likely

Unit 5 Planner
Chapter 13

Use after . . .

LESSON 13.1
Story of My Day

For each student:
- construction paper
- drawing paper
- stapler

LESSON 13.2
About a Minute

For each group:
- Playing Card Master, p. 274
- watch or timer with second hand
- counters

LESSON 13.3
Time Match

For each pair:
- Analog Clock Cards, pp. 249–251
- Digital Clock Cards, pp. 255–257

LESSON 13.4
Time Match
Variation

For each pair:
- Analog Clock Cards, pp. 249–251
- Digital Clock Cards, pp. 255–257

LESSON 13.5
Time for Fun

For each student:
- Time for Fun, p. 177
- Clock Faces, p. 235
- demonstration clock

LESSON 13.6
Story of My Day
Variation

For each student:
- construction paper
- drawing paper
- stapler

LESSON 13.7
Dates and Days

For each pair:
- Dates and Days, p. 178
- Number Cards 1–31, pp. 262–265
- Calendar, p. 234

LESSON 13.8
Favorite Month

For each pair:
- Favorite Month, p. 179
- Calendar, p. 234
- current 12-month calendar

LESSON 13.9
Number of the Week Spotlight on 30

For each student:
- Spotlight on 30, p. 216
- current 12-month calendar

Chapter 13

OBJECTIVES Sequence events in order; identify morning, afternoon, and night

MANAGEMENT Individuals

TIME 20 minutes

MATERIALS
- construction paper
- drawing paper
- stapler

Story of My Day

Before the Activity

Talk with children about some activities that they do in the morning, afternoon, and at night.

Modeling the Activity

Say: **You can make a picture of the story of your day. Think of three things you do each day. Pick one for morning. Pick one for afternoon. Pick one for evening. Make pictures of three things. Draw one picture on each piece of paper.**

When children have completed their pictures, have them describe the activity and tell whether it happens in the morning, afternoon, or night. Then say: **Now put the pictures in order. Write 1, 2, or 3 to show the order. Put your pages together. Make a cover from construction paper and write a title on it. Read the story of your day.**

Helpful Hint

Have children share their booklets with a partner. Encourage children to use the terms *first*, *last*, *before*, and *after* when telling the story of their day.

USE AFTER LESSON 13.2

VOCABULARY

OBJECTIVE Use the vocabulary terms about one minute, less than one minute, and more than one minute in real-life situations

MANAGEMENT Groups

TIME 15 minutes

MATERIALS PER GROUP
- Playing Card Master (p. 274)
- watch or timer with second hand
- counters

About a Minute

Before the Activity

On the cards of the Playing Card Master (p. 274), write the words *about one minute*, *less than one minute*, and *more than one minute*, until you have three sets of three cards each. Work in groups of three. Each child in the group gets one set of three cards.

Modeling the Activity

Say: **We are going to play a game.** Give each child a set of cards and read them aloud with children. Then say: **I am going to give you an activity to do. I will use a stopwatch and tell you when to start the activity and when to stop. Think about how long the activity takes.**

Begin by having children hop on one foot for ten seconds. Say: **Stop. How long do you think you hopped on one foot?** Have children hold up the card that tells how long they think the activity took. Say: **That's right. You hopped on one foot for less than one minute.** Each child that holds up the correct card, gets a counter.

Using the time suggested, start and stop the following activities: putting head on desk (for one minute), coloring a picture (for thirty seconds), writing their names (for fifteen seconds), sitting cross-legged on the floor (for one minute and fifteen seconds), and doing jumping jacks (for twenty seconds). Each time a child gets a correct answer, he or she gets a counter. The activity ends when one child has three counters.

USE AFTER LESSON 13.3

VOCABULARY

OBJECTIVE Tell time to the hour

MANAGEMENT Pairs

TIME 15 minutes

MATERIALS PER PAIR
- Digital Clock Cards (pp. 255–257)
- Analog Clock Cards (pp. 249–251)

Time Match

Before the Activity

From the Digital Clock Cards (pp. 255–257) and the Analog Clock Cards (pp. 249–251), select pairs of cards that show the time to the hour (not the half hour) on analog and digital clocks. Mix the cards.

Modeling the Activity

Say: **We're going to play a matching game. Let's place the cards facedown in rows on the table.** Then say: **I'll turn over a card. What time does it show?** For example, you turn over the card that shows 4:00. Children say the time [4] o'clock. After they respond, say: **I want to turn over another card that shows the same time.** Turn another card face up and ask: **Does this card show the same time as the first one I turned** over? If it does, I've made a match and I'll put those two cards aside. If it doesn't match, I'll turn both cards facedown right where they were. Whether I make a match or not, it's my partner's turn now.

Call on a volunteer to take a turn, and repeat the procedure. Say: **The game is over when all the cards have been matched.**

Helpful Hint

Remind children to watch carefully as the cards are turned over so they can remember where each card is.

USE AFTER LESSON 13.4

OBJECTIVE Tell time to the hour and half hour

Time Match
Variation

Before the Activity

Discuss with the class activities that take about a half hour. Ideas may include: eat a sandwich, walk to school, take a shower.

Modeling the Activity

Repeat "Time Match," as described in Lesson 13.3. Have children play with cards that show the hour and half hour.

USE AFTER LESSON 13.5

VOCABULARY

OBJECTIVE Find elapsed time

MANAGEMENT Individuals

TIME 15 minutes

MATERIALS
• Time for Fun (p. 177)

• Clockfaces (p. 235)

• demonstration clock

Time for Fun

Before the Activity

With a plain piece of paper cover all but the two top clock faces on the clockface master. Photocopy this new page for children to use.

Modeling the Activity

Ask children to think about an activity that they like to do. Guide the discussion to activities that last longer than one hour. Show the clockface and say: **If an activity starts at 3:00, you would draw the clock hands that show 3:00 on the first clock. Now think of the time you would begin your activity.** Have the children draw on their first clock. Ask: **What time would you end this activity? Draw the clock hands on the second clock.** Have the children draw the time on their second clock.

Now, say: **Let's find out how much time has passed from the start of the activity to the end. This is called elapsed time. Suppose your activity began at 3 o'clock and ended at 5 o'clock.** Show a demonstration clock set at 3:00 and move the minute hand around two full circles, counting as you move the clock. Say: **Two hours have elapsed from the start of the activity to the end. Write the number of hours your activity took under the clock faces.** Then encourage children to draw a picture of the activity.

USE AFTER LESSON 13.6

OBJECTIVES Practice telling time; associate the time of day with an activity

Story of My Day
Variation

Before the Activity

Talk with children about some activities they do in the morning, afternoon, and at night.

Modeling the Activity

Repeat "Story of My Day," following the directions on page 84. In this activity, have the children write the time when they would begin each activity. Then have them put the pages in the correct order according to the time.

Helpful Hint

Have children share their booklets with a partner. Encourage the children to tell the times when they begin and end each activity, and how long the activity lasts.

Dates and Days

VOCABULARY

OBJECTIVE Identify and order the days of the week

MANAGEMENT Pairs

TIME 15 minutes

MATERIALS PER PAIR
- Dates and Days (p. 178)
- Number Cards (pp. 262–265)
- Calendar (p. 234)

Before the Activity

Select only the Number Cards (pp. 262–265) that correspond to the number of days in the current month. Write the name of the current month at the top of the Calendar (p. 234). You may either number the days on the Calendar before you copy it for children's use, or guide children in writing in the numbers themselves.

Modeling the Activity

Show children the Calendar and explain that it shows this month. Lead children in saying the days of the week in order. Ask a volunteer to pick a Number Card and read the number aloud. Say: **Find the day with that number. What day of the week is that date?** Show the day of the week for that date. Then say: **Now it is my turn to pick a Number Card and tell the day of the week for the date.** Continue, taking one or two more turns.

Helpful Hint

To find the day of the week, suggest that children put their finger on the number on the Calendar, and then move the finger up the column until they reach the day.

Favorite Month

VOCABULARY

OBJECTIVES Identify the months; determine which day represents tomorrow

MANAGEMENT Pairs

TIME 20 minutes

MATERIALS PER PAIR
- Favorite Month (p. 179)
- Calendar (p. 234)
- current calendar showing all the months

Before the Activity

Copy the Calendar (p. 234) for each child.

Modeling the Activity

Display a large calendar for this year. Say: **Let's say all the months of the year together.** Then ask: **What is your favorite month?** Have children tell why they chose that month. Distribute a blank Calendar and have children write the name of their favorite month at the top. Demonstrate how to fill in the month.

Say, for example: **My favorite month is August. My birthday is August 5.** Let a volunteer draw a picture for your birthday on the Calendar. Suggest other activities you like to do in that month and have volunteers write them in on the days you have designated.

After five days are filled in, point to a "filled" day and ask: **What day is this? Suppose this day is today, what day will it be tomorrow?**

Let children work in pairs to complete their Calendars. Then have them share their Calendar with the class.

Helpful Hint

If the children need help filling in days on their Calendars, let them brainstorm favorite activities and discuss on what days of the month they do each activity.

USE AFTER LESSON 13.9

NUMBER OF THE WEEK
Spotlight on 30

NUMBER SENSE

OBJECTIVE Use the number 30 to solve problems in many contexts

MANAGEMENT Individuals

TIME 15 minutes

MATERIALS
- Spotlight on 30 (p. 216)
- current 12-month calendar

Modeling the Activity

Show children Spotlight on 30 (p. 216). Say: **Today we will explore some ways you can use the number 30.** Read the first activity and have volunteers suggest activities they could do in 30 minutes.

Ask a volunteer to read the other activities to the class. After each set of directions, give children the items they need to complete the exercise, before moving on to the next activity.

Helpful Hint

Ask volunteers to share their solutions. Children should realize that pencils are longer than erasers, so 30 pencils would be longer than 30 erasers.

Answers

1. *Answers may vary. Sample:* make dinner, read a book, go for a walk

2. April, June, September, November

3. 26, 28, 32

4. 30 new pencils placed end to end

Unit 5 Planner
Chapter 14

Use after . . .

LESSON 14.1
Money Bags

For each group:
- coin sets (pennies, nickels, and dimes)
- plastic bags
- index cards

LESSON 14.2
How Many Coins?

For each pair:
- How Many Coins?, p. 180
- 4-Part Spinner, p. 278
- Money Workmat, pp. 282–283
- coin sets (pennies and nickels)

LESSON 14.3
How Many Coins?
Variation

For each pair:
- How Many Coins?, p. 180
- 4-Part Spinner, p. 278
- Money Workmat, pp. 282–283
- coin sets (pennies, nickels, and dimes)

LESSON 14.4
Shopping Spree

For each pair:
- Shopping Spree, p. 181
- Class Store Cards (19¢–45¢), pp. 252–254
- coin sets (pennies, nickels, and dimes)

LESSON 14.5
Great Coin Count

For each group:
- Great Coin Count Gameboard, pp. 294–295
- coin sets (pennies, nickels, and dimes)
- paper bag
- game pieces

LESSON 14.6
Two Ways to Pay
Cross-Curricular

For each pair:
- Class Store Cards, pp. 252–254
- Fan Gameboard, pp. 292–293
- coin sets (pennies, nickels, and dimes)
- counters

LESSON 14.7
Number of the Week Spotlight on 25

For each student:
- Spotlight on 25, p. 217

Chapter 14

USE AFTER LESSON 14.1

VOCABULARY

OBJECTIVES Identify coins and their value; count groups of like coins: pennies, nickels, dimes

MANAGEMENT Groups

TIME 20 minutes

MATERIALS PER GROUP
- coin sets
- plastic bags
- index cards

Money Bags

Before the Activity

Fill plastic bags with like coins: 10–15 pennies, 1–10 nickels, or 1–7 dimes. Make a card that shows the amount in each bag. Display the cards face up.

Modeling the Activity

Review counting by 5s and 10s. Review the amounts on the cards. Hold up the 5¢ card and ask: **What coin has the value of 5¢?** Have a volunteer hold up a nickel. Continue with 1¢ and 10¢. Tell children they will match the value of groups of like coins to each card.

Empty the contents of one bag onto the table. Say: **What coins are on the table? [nickels] What amount can you count on by to find the total value of the [nickels]?** Have children count on by 5s. Now have a child find the amount card with the matching value. Remind children that having a greater number of coins does not always mean having a greater total value.

Continue until each child has had a turn. Ask: **Did you choose the same total value card when counting different coins? Why?** Discuss that there are different ways to show the same amount.

How Many Coins?

OBJECTIVES Identify a nickel and its value; count nickels and pennies

MANAGEMENT Pairs

TIME 15 minutes

MATERIALS PER PAIR
- How Many Coins? (p. 180)
- 2 Blank Spinners (p. 276)
- Money Workmat (pp. 282–283)
- coin sets (pennies and nickels)

Before the Activity

Label the Blank Spinners 1, 2, 3, and 4 (p. 276). Prepare sets of 15 pennies and 10 nickels for each pair.

Modeling the Activity

Hold up a penny and say: **Name the coin. What is the value?** Repeat with a nickel. Place the pennies and nickels on the Money Workmat (pp. 282–283).

Have a child help you demonstrate "How Many Coins?" Say: **Partners take turns spinning the spinner.** Have the child spin the spinner and say the number. [3] Then say: **Take [3] pennies from the mat.** Continue taking turns. When one partner has five pennies say: **Place the pennies back on the mat and trade them for a nickel.** Each time a player adds one nickel to his or her pile, say: **Count the total value of your coins. Write the amount.** Remind children to count the coin with the greatest value first.

Continue to take turns until each player has five nickels. Say: **The game is over when each player has five nickels.**

How Many Coins?
Variation

OBJECTIVES Identify a dime and its value; count dimes, nickels, and pennies

MANAGEMENT Pairs

TIME 20 minutes

MATERIALS PER PAIR
- 2 Blank Spinners (p. 276)
- Money Workmat (pp. 282–283)
- coin sets

Before the Activity

Repeat "How Many Coins?" as described in Lesson 14.2. Vary the activity by using dimes as well as nickels and pennies. Prepare 2 Blank Spinners (p. 276) and sets of coins as follows: 15 pennies, 5 nickels, and 8 to 10 dimes. Display the Money Workmat (pp. 282–283).

Modeling the Activity

Play "How Many Coins?" following the directions in that activity. Have children trade five pennies for one nickel and two nickels for one dime. The game is over when each child has four dimes.

OBJECTIVE Use coins to show amounts of money and find the total value

MANAGEMENT Pairs

TIME 15 minutes

MATERIALS PER PAIR
- Shopping Spree (p. 181)
- Class Store Cards (19¢–45¢) (pp. 252–254)
- coin sets

Shopping Spree

Before the Activity

Prepare and display the Class Store Cards (pp. 252–254) face up on the table.

Modeling the Activity

Focus attention on the Class Store Cards. Describe a few of the cards and then mix the cards and place them facedown in a pile. Tell children they will go on a shopping spree. Have a child choose a card. Say: **Read the price of an item. Pay the store clerk (your partner) with the correct amount.** Ask: **How much does the item cost?** Have the child use their coins to find the value. Remind children to begin counting with the coin of the greatest value.

Have children continue to take turns being the customer and the store clerk. Both partners count the coins to check the amount. If the customer pays with the correct amount, then he or she keeps the card. Then the child returns the coins to the pile. Children continue to play until all the items have been bought.

> **Helpful Hint**

You may want to review counting by 1s, 5s, and 10s.

OBJECTIVE Identify combinations of coins that equal 25 cents

MANAGEMENT Groups

TIME 15 minutes

MATERIALS PER GROUP
- The Great Coin Count Gameboard (pp. 294–295)
- coin sets (pennies, nickels, dimes)
- paper bag
- game pieces

The Great Coin Count

Before the Activity

Place coin sets into a bag for each group. Have children select their game piece.

Modeling the Activity

Display the gameboard and say: **Begin at 1¢. Read the money values in each circle.** Point to each circle as the children count. Tell children they will pull coins out of a bag and move around the gameboard until they reach 25¢.

Have the first player take a coin out of the bag. Say: **Name the coin. [nickel] What is the value? [5 cents] Move [5] spaces forward.** Direct the child to begin at 1¢. After the child moves, say: **Leave your game piece on the board. Place your coin in a pile in front of you.** Children take turns repeating the steps. Be sure that children count on to move forward from the space on which they last landed.

Continue playing. When children reach the 25¢ space, say: **You must have the exact amount to land on the 25¢ space.** Explain that if children pick a coin that would put them beyond 25¢, they return the coin to the bag. The turn passes to the next player. Players continue until all children reach 25¢. Each child shows what coins they use to find the total value of 25¢. Discuss how different coins can be used to show the same value.

USE AFTER LESSON 14.6

CROSS-CURRICULAR
Social Studies

OBJECTIVE Use different coins to represent a given amount of money

MANAGEMENT Pairs

TIME 15 minutes

MATERIALS PER PAIR
- Class Store Cards (pp. 252–254)
- Fan Gameboard (pp. 292–293)
- coin sets (pennies, nickels, and dimes)
- counters

Two Ways to Pay

Before the Activity
Prepare sets of Class Store Cards (pp. 252–254). Mix up the cards. Display these with the Fan Gameboard (pp. 292–293).

Modeling the Activity
Review the penny, nickel, and dime. Have children identify each coin. Then have them tell the value of each coin. Say: **A nickel is worth 5¢. Can you show 5¢ using different coins?** Tell children they will use different coin combinations to "buy" an item.

Play the customer and choose a partner to play the store clerk. Place the coin sets on the table. Say: **Place the cards facedown in a pile. Now choose the top card.** Say: **Name the item. How much does it cost?** After telling the cost, have the partner show the amount with coins. Say: **Now I will show the same amount using different coins.** Encourage children to use coins other than just pennies whenever possible.

Partners count coins to check. If the new combination of coins is the same amount, say: **I have different coins to show the same amount, so I put a counter on my fan.**

Children take turns being the customer and the store clerk. Game ends when one fan is full.

Helpful Hint
Remind children that they can look at the group of coins the "store clerk" used to show the amount and then trade coins to make different combinations.

USE AFTER LESSON 14.7

NUMBER OF THE WEEK
Spotlight on 25

NUMBER SENSE

OBJECTIVE Use the number 25 to solve problems in many contexts

MANAGEMENT Individuals

TIME 15 minutes

MATERIALS
• Spotlight on 25 (p. 217)

Before the Activity

Make a copy of Spotlight on 25 (p. 217) for each child.

Modeling the Activity

Show children the Spotlight on 25 sheet. Say: **Today we will explore different ways to use the number 25.** Read the first exercise and say: **Find the number pattern.** Have children count by fives as they fill in the missing numbers. Then have them write the missing numbers on the page.

Give each child a copy of Spotlight on 25. Read the other exercises to the class. After each set of directions, give children time to complete the exercise before moving on to the next set of directions. Allow time to discuss Exercise 4.

Answers

1. 15; 25

2. Greta

3. Wednesday, May 25

4. 2 nickels

Unit 6 Planner
Chapter 15

Use after . . .

LESSON 15.1	**LESSON 15.2**	**LESSON 15.3**	**LESSON 15.4**
How Many? *Variation*	**Shake in Step**	**Part Plus Part**	**Part Plus Part** *Variation*
For each pair: • How Many?, p. 152 • Number Cards 5–9, p. 262 • twelve 2-color counters • plastic cup	For each pair: • Shake in Step, p. 182 • 10 × 10 Grid Paper, p. 228 • ten 2-color counters	For each student: • Part-Part-Whole Workmat, pp. 284–285 • Number Cards 1–10, pp. 262–263 • 11 counters • teacher-made worksheet	For each student: • Part-Part-Whole Workmat, pp. 284–285 • Number Cards 1–10, pp. 262–263 • 11 counters • teacher-made worksheet
LESSON 15.5	**LESSON 15.6**	**LESSON 15.7**	**LESSON 15.8**
Domino Match	**Three in a Row**	**Pick a Part**	**Number of the Week Spotlight on 12**
For each group: • Domino Cards, pp. 258–260	For each student: • Three in a Row, p. 183 • 4-Part Spinner, p. 278 • crayons	For each student: • Pick a Part, p. 184 • Part-Part-Whole Workmat, pp. 284–285 • Playing Card Master, p. 274 • counters	For each student: • Spotlight on 12, p. 218

Chapter 15

USE AFTER LESSON 15.1

OBJECTIVE Count on by 1, 2, and 3 to solve addition facts through 12

How Many?
Variation

Repeat the game "How Many?" (p. 37). Do the activity in the same way, but use Number Cards 5–9 (pp. 262–263), a plastic cup, and 12 two-sided counters.

USE AFTER LESSON 15.2

OBJECTIVE Use counters on a ten frame to make sums of 10

MANAGEMENT Pairs

TIME 15 minutes

MATERIALS PER PAIR
- Shake in Step (p. 182)
- 10 × 10 Grid Paper (p. 228)
- ten 2-color counters

Shake in Step

Before the Activity

Use the 10 × 10 Grid Paper to create the game board shown below. Have the children color the first circle above the problems red and the second circle yellow.

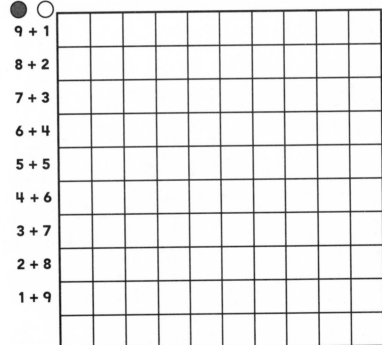

Modeling the Activity

Say: **In this game, you are going to use 2-colored counters to show ways to make a sum of ten.**

Demonstrate how to play by shaking ten counters and then spilling them on a table. Say, for example: **I got three reds and seven yellows. So I will find the problem that matches my counters.** Point to where the sum 3 (red) + 7 (yellow) is on the game board. Say: **Now I am going to color in three red squares and then seven yellow squares in this row.** Color three red squares and then seven yellow squares in the appropriate row.

Remind children that in this activity, three yellow and seven red is not the same as seven red and three yellow. Although added together both give ten, the coloring pattern will be different.

Tell the children that when they play the game, whoever spills the counters also colors in the row. If a fact is already colored in, the person who spilled the counters loses a turn. Have children keep playing until they find all the facts. When children are finished they should have a stair step pattern on their paper if they have done the activity correctly.

USE AFTER LESSON 15.3

Part Plus Part

OBJECTIVE Solve problems using addition facts through 11

MANAGEMENT Individuals

TIME 15 minutes

MATERIALS

- Part-Part-Whole Workmat (pp. 284–285)

- Number Cards 1–10 (pp. 262–263)

- 11 counters

- teacher-made worksheet

Before the Activity

Copy and cut Number Cards 1–10. Prepare a worksheet by writing the numbers one to ten down the left-hand side of the page. To the right of each number, write a plus sign. Leave room for children to write an addend, an equal sign, and a sum for each number. Copy for the children's use.

Whole	
Part	**Part**

```
1 +
2 +
3 +
4 +
5 +
6 +
7 +
8 +
9 +
10 +
```

Modeling the Activity

Show the worksheet. Say: **We are going to find facts for 11.** Put 11 counters in the *whole* section of the mat as children count along. Mix the Number Cards and put them facedown in a pile.

Say: **I'll start by picking the top card.** Pick up the card and show it. Ask: **What number does this card show? [four] Yes, it's a four. I'll put four counters on one *part* section of the mat.** Move four counters to one of the *part* sections.

Then say: **Now I'll put the rest of the counters on the other *part* section of the mat.** Have children count along as you move the other counters. **There are seven counters in this *part*. How many counters did I put in the first *part* section? Yes, four, so I look for the 4 on my paper.** Hold up the worksheet and point to the line on which is written 4 +. **How many counters are in the other *part* section? Seven, so I write a 7 after the plus sign. Now what's my sum? Let's move all the counters into the *whole* section and count to check.** After you have moved the counters say: **Now I'll finish my addition sentence by writing an equal sign and an 11.**

Children can work independently to complete their worksheets. Tell them to keep going until all the lines are filled.

Helpful Hint

Make sure children move all their counters back into the *whole* section when they write each addition sentence, so they will be ready to start the next one.

USE AFTER LESSON 15.4

OBJECTIVE Solve problems using addition facts through 12

Part Plus Part
Variation

Begin by explaining that we call 12 objects one dozen. Say: **Eggs are bought by the dozen. That means there are 12 eggs in the box.**

Repeat "Part Plus Part" (p. 98), using 12 counters. Do the activity in the same way but use Number Cards 1–11. The numbers on the side of the paper go from one to eleven. Use 12 counters.

USE AFTER LESSON 15.5

Domino Match

OBJECTIVE Solve addition facts through 12

MANAGEMENT Groups

TIME 15 minutes

MATERIALS PER GROUP
• Domino Cards
  (pp. 258–260)

Before the Activity

Arrange the Domino Cards in four rows facedown.

Modeling the Activity

Begin by showing children the rows of Domino Cards. Say: **We're going to play Domino Match.** Call on a volunteer to turn over two cards. Say: **Add the dots on one card. What is the sum of the dots on this card?** Point to one of the face up cards. Ask: **What is the sum of the dots on this card?** Point to the other face up card. Say: **If both cards have the same sum, you can pick them up and take another turn. If they don't have the same sum, turn the cards back over and leave them in the same place.**

Continue the game by having other children turn over two cards at a time, add up the number of dots, and determine if the cards match. Continue until all of the cards have been picked up.

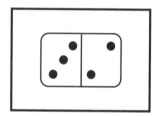 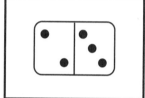

Helpful Hint

Remind children to watch as other players turn over cards. This will give them clues for matching cards when it's their turn.

USE AFTER LESSON 15.6

Three in a Row

OBJECTIVE Add 3 addends up to sums of 12

MANAGEMENT Individual

TIME 15 minutes

MATERIALS
• Three in a Row (p. 183)

• Blank Spinner (p. 276)

• crayons

Before the Activity

Use the Blank Spinner (p. 276) to create a spinner divided into quarters. Number the sections 1 to 4.

Modeling the Activity

Tell children that they will be adding three numbers and coloring shapes. Ask a volunteer to begin by spinning the spinner. Ask: **What number is the spinner pointing to?** Say: **Write that number at the bottom of your paper. Make**

a plus sign after the number. Have the child spin again.
Say: **Write the number the spinner is pointing to after the plus sign. Then write another plus sign.** Have the child spin a third time. Say: **Write the number the spinner is pointing to after the plus sign. Then write an equal sign.**

Have the child draw and color shapes above the addition problem to represent each addend. Invite the child to use the shapes to help determine the sum and write it to complete the addition sentence.

Have the children repeat the activity several times. Then have them share their addition sentences at the chalkboard.

USE AFTER LESSON 15.7

OBJECTIVE Find the missing addend

MANAGEMENT Individuals

TIME 10 minutes

MATERIALS
- Pick a Part (p. 184)
- Part-Part-Whole Workmat (pp. 284–285)
- Playing Card Master (p. 274)
- counters

Pick a Part

Before the Activity

Copy the Part-Part-Whole Workmat (pp. 284–285). Prepare cards from the Playing Card Master (p. 274). On each card, write an addition sentence with a blank in place of the second addend. You may want to use these number sentences:

$9 + \square = 12; \quad 7 + \square = 12; \quad 6 + \square = 11;$

$8 + \square = 12; \quad 4 + \square = 11; \quad 9 + \square = 11$

Modeling the Activity

Show the cards you have prepared and explain that children will use the Part-Part-Whole Workmat and the counters to find the missing numbers. Call on a volunteer to demonstrate as you explain. Say: **Pick one of the cards. Look at the addition problem on the card. What is the sum? Put that many counters in the *whole* section of the mat. What are you trying to find? How can you find it?** Prompt children to put counters representing the first addend in the first *part* section, and the rest of the counters in the second *part* section, to find the missing number.

Have children work independently to solve the problems on all the cards.

Helpful Hint

To help children keep track of the two addends, suggest that they put the card below the Part-Part-Whole Workmat so the plus lines up with the line between the two *part* sections. This may help them see that the counters in the right-hand *part* section show the number that goes in the box.

USE AFTER LESSON 15.8

Number of the Week
Spotlight on 12

NUMBER SENSE

OBJECTIVE Use the number 12 to solve problems in many contexts

MANAGEMENT Individuals

TIME 15 minutes

MATERIALS
• Spotlight on 12 (p. 218)

Modeling the Activity

Show children the Spotlight on 12 sheet (p. 218). Say: **Today we will explore some different ways that you can use the number 12.** Read the first exercise. Ask the children how they would find out how many balloons each child gets.

Ask a volunteer to read the other exercises to the class. After each set of directions, give children time to complete the exercise before moving on to the next set of directions.

Ask volunteers to talk about Exercise 4 and how they know that there are 24 eggs in 2 dozen. Have them show how they would use pictures or counters to solve the problem.

Answers

1. Children draw 2 nickels, 2 pennies; 2 pennies

2. 12

3. 7

4. 6 eggs; *Answers may vary. Sample:* I used the double 6 and 6 to make 12 eggs.

Unit 6 Planner
Chapter 16

Use after . . .

LESSON 16.1	**LESSON 16.2**	**LESSON 16.3**	**LESSON 16.4**
Along the Line *Variation*	**Hidden Numbers**	**Hidden Numbers** *Variation*	**Roll It Out** *Variation* *Cross-Curricular*
For each pair: • Along the Line, p. 155 • Number Lines, p. 240 • 6-Part Spinner, p. 279 • 2 counters	For each pair: • Hidden Numbers, p. 185 • Number Cards 1–11, pp. 262–263 • 11 counters • small box	For each pair: • Hidden Numbers, p. 185 • Number Cards 1–11, pp. 262–263 • 11 counters • small box	For each pair: • Part-Part-Whole Workmat, pp. 284–285 • Part-Part-Whole Sheet, p. 241 • number cube • 10 counters

LESSON 16.5	**LESSON 16.6**	**LESSON 16.7**	**LESSON 16.8**
Family in Counters	**Family in Counters** *Variation*	**What's in a Name?**	**Number of the Week Spotlight on 11**
For each student: • Family in Counters, p. 186 • Playing Card Master, p. 274 • eleven 2-sided counters • cup	For each student: • Family in Counters, p. 186 • Playing Card Master, p. 274 • eleven 2-sided counters • cup	For each pair: • What's in a Name?, p. 187 • Addition Facts Through 12, p. 229 • Subtraction Facts Through 12, p. 246	For each student: • Spotlight on 11, p. 219 • Part-Part-Whole Workmat, pp. 284–285

Chapter 16

OBJECTIVE Use a number line and other strategies to subtract with facts through 12

Along the Line
Variation

Before the Activity

Repeat "Along the Line," as described on page 42. Vary the activity by labeling one 6-Part Spinner (p. 279) 1–6 and the other 7–12. Prepare three Blank Number Lines (p. 240) on the Number Line Sheet from 0–12.

Modeling the Activity

Play "Along the Line," but use the number lines to subtract with facts through 12.

OBJECTIVE Solve subtraction problems using subtraction facts through 11

MANAGEMENT Pairs

TIME 15 minutes

MATERIALS PER PAIR
• Hidden Numbers (p. 185)

• Number Cards 1–11 (pp. 262–263)

• 11 counters

• small box

Hidden Numbers

Before the Activity

Draw a Part-Part-Whole Workmat on the board. Write *11* in the Whole section. Prepare Number Cards 1–11 (pp. 262–263). Mix the cards and place them facedown in a pile.

Modeling the Activity

Focus attention on the Part-Part-Whole Workmat. Tell children they will use counters to model subtracting from 11. Have a child help you demonstrate. Place 11 counters on the table. Choose a card. Say: **Cover your eyes while I place some of the counters under the box.** Have your partner uncover his or her eyes and ask: **How many counters do you see?** Write this number on the board. Then ask: **How many counters are hidden under the box?** Remind children to count back from the whole to find the other part. Lift the box to verify the answer. Complete the Part-Part-Whole Workmat.

Have partners take turns hiding counters and completing the subtraction. Suggest they may want to change the number of counters that they begin with.

Hidden Numbers
Variation

OBJECTIVE Solve subtraction facts through 12

Before the Activity

Repeat "Hidden Numbers" as described on page 104. Vary the activity by placing the Number Cards (pp. 262–263) in two piles: 1–11 and 8–12. Copy Part-Part-Whole Sheets (p. 241) for each pair.

Modeling the Activity

Play "Hidden Numbers." Choose a child and say: **Pick a Number Card 8–12. Place that number of counters next to the box.** Then continue the activity as described in "Hidden Numbers." Children will subtract from 12 or less. Have children record numbers on the Part-Part-Whole Sheets. Then say the related facts for each subtraction.

Roll It Out
Variation

CROSS-CURRICULAR Social Studies

OBJECTIVE Solving related addition and subtraction problems through 12

Before the Activity

Repeat "Roll It Out," as described on page 44. Vary the activity by using a number cube 1–6. Create a story about using a recipe to make apple pies.

Modeling the Activity

Help children create the first related addition and subtraction story. For example say: **The baker at the restaurant is making apple pie. She needs to use two types of apples: Cortland and Granny Smith.** Roll the cube to find how many of each. Have children continue by creating and modeling their own stories.

OBJECTIVE Write fact families for 11

MANAGEMENT Individual

TIME 15 minutes

MATERIALS
- Family in Counters (p. 186)
- Playing Card Master (p. 274)
- eleven 2-sided counters
- cup

Family in Counters

Before the Activity

Make a copy of the Playing Card Master (p. 274) for each child. Display the cup and counters.

Modeling the Activity

Focus attention on the eleven counters. Say: **Count how many.** Then put the counters in a cup. Gently shake the cup and spill the counters onto the table. Tell children they are going to write a fact family using the counters. Guide the children to write the first addition fact. Write a blank addition sentence on the card. Ask: **How many counters are red?** Write the number in the sentence. Continue and ask: **How many counters are yellow? How many counters do we have all together?** Complete the fact.

Choose a volunteer and say: **Look at the counters. Write a related fact under the first one.** Remind children that there are only three numbers in a fact family. Keep asking until you have all four facts. Be sure children record the fact family in one box on the playing card master.

OBJECTIVE Write fact families for 12

Family in Counters
Variation

Before the Activity

Repeat "Family in Counters." Vary the activity by using 12 counters and have children play in pairs.

Modeling the Activity

Repeat "Family in Counters," but have one child write the addition facts and the partner write the subtraction facts in a family.

What's in a Name?

Teacher Notes

VOCABULARY

OBJECTIVE Find names for the same number

MANAGEMENT Pairs

TIME 15 minutes

MATERIALS PER PAIR
- What's in a Name? (p. 187)
- Addition Facts Through 12 (p. 229)
- Subtraction Facts Through 12 (p. 246)

Before the Activity

Prepare Addition Facts Through 12 (p. 229) and Subtraction Facts Through 12 (p. 246) for each pair.

Modeling the Activity

Display one pair of cards that name the same number. Review *sums*, *differences*, and *names for numbers*. Ask a volunteer to solve the addition or subtraction on both cards. Say: **They are both names for the same number.** Ask: **Can you write another name for this number?** Have the child write it on a blank card. Mix the cards and place them facedown on the table.

Choose a volunteer to help you demonstrate the game. Say: **Turn over two cards.** Ask the volunteer to solve the addition or subtraction on each card. Ask: **Do the two cards name the same number?** If the cards name the same number, say: **Keep both cards. Take another turn.** This continues until he or she pulls two cards that do *not* name the same number. If the cards do not name the same number they are returned to the table facedown. Children continue taking turns for as long as time allows or until all the cards are gone.

Helpful Hint

You might want to have children make a new card each time they find a pair that names the same number.

NUMBER OF THE WEEK
Spotlight on 11

Before the Activity

Make a copy of Spotlight on 11 (p. 219) for each child. Display counters and a Part-Part-Whole Workmat (pp. 284–285). Remind children they can use counters on a Part-Part-Whole Workmat to help them model the subtraction.

Modeling the Activity

Show children the Spotlight on 11 sheet. Say: **Today we will explore different ways to use the number 11.** Read the first activity. Say: **Count how many circles. Now count how many squares. Subtract to find the difference.**

Give each child a copy of Spotlight on 11. Read the other exercises to the class. After each set of directions, give children time to complete the exercise before moving on to the next set of directions.

Answers

1. 5 circles

2. 11:00

3. $2 + 9 = 11$; $9 + 2 = 11$; $11 - 9 = 2$; $11 - 2 = 9$

4. No; *Answers may vary. Sample:* Eleven is an odd number and an odd number of counters cannot be divided evenly between two children.

NUMBER SENSE

OBJECTIVE Use the number 11 to solve problems in many contexts

MANAGEMENT Individuals

TIME 15 minutes

MATERIALS
- Spotlight on 11 (p. 219)
- Part-Part-Whole Workmat (pp. 284–285)

Unit 7 Planner
Chapter 17

Use after . . .

LESSON 17.1

Taller or Shorter
Cross-Curricular

For each pair:
- 2-Column Chart, p. 226
- connecting cubes
- plants and other objects to compare

LESSON 17.2

Guess and Measure

For each student:
- Guess and Measure, p. 188
- 3-Column Chart, p. 227
- various small objects, such as paint brush, box of crayons, eraser, pencil, pen, pad of drawing paper
- 20 connecting cubes

LESSON 17.3

List the Lengths

For each pair:
- List the Lengths, p. 189
- 3-Column Chart, p. 227
- Number Cards 1–20, pp. 262–264
- classroom objects to measure

LESSON 17.4

List the Lengths
Variation

For each pair:
- List the Lengths, p. 189
- 3-Column Chart, p. 227
- Number Cards 1–20, pp. 262–264
- classroom objects to measure

LESSON 17.5

Weighing In
Cross-Curricular

For each pair:
- Weighing In, p. 190
- pan balance
- chalkboard eraser
- crayons
- connecting cubes

LESSON 17.6

Weighing In
Variation 1

For each pair:
- Weighing In, p. 190
- pan balance
- chalkboard eraser
- crayons
- connecting cubes

LESSON 17.7

Weighing In
Variation 2

For each pair:
- Weighing In, p. 190
- pan balance
- chalkboard eraser
- crayons
- connecting cubes

LESSON 17.8

Number of the Week Spotlight on 24

For each student:
- Spotlight on 24, p. 220

Chapter 17

CROSS-CURRICULAR
Science

OBJECTIVE Compare the height of two objects

MANAGEMENT Pairs

TIME 15 minutes

MATERIALS PER PAIR
- 2-Column Chart (p. 226)
- connecting cubes
- plants and other objects to compare

Taller or Shorter

Before the Activity

Label the columns of the 2-Column Chart (p. 226) *taller* and *shorter*. Copy. Give each pair of children nine cubes. Have objects available for children to compare.

Modeling the Activity

Say: **Sometimes scientists need to measure plants to see how they are growing. Today you are going to compare plants and other objects to the length of your cubes.**

Demonstrate how to compare by showing a plant and the connecting cubes. Ask: **Do you think the plant is taller than or shorter than the cubes?** After the children have made their guesses, show them how to line up their cubes with the plant to compare the height. Then show children how to record the result on the chart by drawing a small picture of the plant in the correct column.

Have children take turns finding an object that is taller than the cubes and an object that is shorter. Tell them to make a guess before they do the comparison. Remind them to draw a picture of the plant or object.

OBJECTIVE Estimate and measure length using nonstandard units

MANAGEMENT Individuals

TIME 15 minutes

MATERIALS PER PAIR
- Guess and Measure (p. 188)
- 3-Column Chart (p. 227)
- various small objects, such as paintbrush, box of crayons, eraser, pencil, pen, pad of drawing paper
- 20 connecting cubes

Guess and Measure

Before the Activity

Label the 3-Column Chart (p. 227) with the following heads: *Object, Estimate,* and *Measure*. Copy for children's use.

Modeling the Activity

Show children the paintbrush. Say: **We're going to estimate and then measure the length of some things. First, I'll draw the paintbrush in column 1.** Point to column 1 on the 3-Column Chart. Then say: **This can be measured in cubes.** Point to connecting cubes. **How long do you think it is in cubes?** Wait for an answer, and then say: **Let's write your estimate in column 2.** Write the estimate and say: **Now let's measure to find out.** Have a volunteer measure the paintbrush in cubes. Then say, for example: **This paintbrush is about nine cubes long.** Write the measure in column 3.

Have children continue choosing objects, drawing them, estimating their lengths, measuring with cubes, and recording their estimates and measures on the chart.

Helpful Hints

1. Remind children to measure the actual objects, not their drawings of the objects.

2. Remind children that an estimate is a good guess and that an estimate cannot be wrong.

USE AFTER LESSON 17.3

OBJECTIVES Estimate length and height in inches; measure to the nearest inch

MANAGEMENT Pairs

TIME 15 minutes

MATERIALS PER PAIR
- List the Lengths (p. 189)
- 3-Column Chart (p. 227)
- Number Cards 1–12 (pp. 262–263)
- inch ruler
- classroom objects to measure

List the Lengths

Before the Activity

Label the 3-Column Chart (p. 227) from left to right as follows: *Number, Object,* and *Length.* Copy for children's use. Select Number Cards 1–12 (pp. 262–263) for each pair of children.

Modeling the Activity

Show children the number cards. Say: **I'm going to work with a partner to find things of a certain length.** Pick up the number card with 5 and say: **Our number is 5. Let's write the number 5 in column 1.** Point to column 1 on the 3-Column Chart. Ask: **What object is about 5 inches long?** Have your partner find something that is about 5 inches long. Then say: **List that object in column 2. Now let's measure to be sure.** Wait for your partner to measure the object mentioned. Then say: **Write the number of inches in column 3.** Have children continue to estimate, measure, and record answers.

Helpful Hint

If there are not enough 1- to 12-inch objects available, provide different lengths of construction-paper strips.

USE AFTER LESSON 17.4

OBJECTIVE Estimate length and height in centimeters to measure to the nearest centimeter

List the Lengths
Variation

Repeat "List the Lengths." Copy Number Cards 1–12 (pp. 262–263). Have children measure in centimeters.

Say: **Today we are going to estimate the length and height in centimeters. You will need a centimeter ruler.**

Helpful Hint

If there are not enough 1- to 20-centimeter objects available, provide different lengths of construction-paper strips.

CROSS-CURRICULAR Science

OBJECTIVE Use non-standard units to measure weight

MANAGEMENT Pairs

TIME 15 minutes

MATERIALS PER PAIR
- Weighing In (p. 190)
- pan balance
- chalkboard eraser
- crayons
- connecting cubes

Weighing In

Before the Activity

Make sure you have enough crayons to equal the weight of the eraser.

Modeling the Activity

Say: **When you go to the store, you often have to weigh what you buy. Today we are going to practice weighing things.** Put the eraser on one side of the pan balance and ask: **Do you think we'll need to put a lot of crayons on the other side of the balance to weigh the same as the eraser?**

Put a few crayons on the other side of the pan balance. Ask: **Do I need more crayons, or do I need fewer?** Add or subtract crayons according to children's answers.

Have children complete the experiment on their own.

(**Helpful Hint**)

If a chalkboard eraser is not available, use an object of approximately equal weight. You could also use markers instead of crayons.

OBJECTIVES Introduce the pound as a unit of measure; measure weight in pounds

Weighing In
Variation 1

Repeat "Weighing In." Use a 1-pound weight or a 1-pound bag of coffee. Have children compare objects to the 1-pound weight to determine whether the object is *more than* or *less than* 1 pound.

Say: **Today we are going to weigh objects to find out if they weigh 1 pound.** Let children hold the pound weight.

OBJECTIVES Introduce the kilogram as a unit of measure; measure mass in kilograms

Weighing In
Variation 2

Repeat "Weighing In." Use a kilogram mass or an equivalent. Have children compare objects to 1 kilogram.

You might want to mention that the kilogram is a unit of measure that is used in other countries more than in our country.

NUMBER OF THE WEEK
Spotlight on 24

NUMBER SENSE

OBJECTIVE Use the number 24 to solve problems in many contexts

MANAGEMENT Individuals

TIME 15 minutes

MATERIALS
• Spotlight on 24 (p. 220)

Modeling the Activity

Show children the Spotlight on 24 sheet (p. 220). Say: **Today we will explore some different ways that you can use the number 24.** Read the first problem. Ask the children what the pattern is. Have them count by 2s backwards with you, saying the missing numbers. Then have them write the missing numbers.

Ask a volunteer to read the other exercises to the class. After each set of directions, give children time to complete the exercise before moving on to the next set of directions.

Ask volunteers to explain their thinking for Exercise 4.

Answers

1. 24; 20

2. Linda

3. 24

4. taller

Unit 7 Planner
Chapter 18

Use after . . .

LESSON 18.1
More or Less

For each pair:
- More or Less, p. 191
- various containers
- scoop
- uncooked rice

LESSON 18.2
More or Less
Variation 1

For each pair:
- More or Less, p. 191
- various containers
- scoop
- uncooked rice

LESSON 18.3
More or Less
Variation 2

For each pair:
- More or Less, p. 191
- various containers
- scoop
- uncooked rice

LESSON 18.4
Dress for Success

For each student:
- Dress for Success, p. 192
- Story Mat, p. 244
- oaktag

LESSON 18.5
**Number of the Week
Spotlight on 37**

For each student
- Spotlight on 37, p. 221

Chapter 18

USE AFTER LESSON 18.1

OBJECTIVE Order and compare the capacity of containers

MANAGEMENT Pairs

TIME 15 minutes

MATERIALS PER PAIR
- More or Less (p. 191)
- various containers
- scoop
- uncooked rice

More or Less

Before the Activity
Gather containers of various sizes, such as mugs, pitchers, jars, cans, pots, bowls, and so on.

Modeling the Activity
Have a volunteer use a scoop to fill a container with rice. Then have the volunteer choose another container of a different size. Ask: **Will the second container hold more or less than the first one?** After children answer, say: **I think you are right, but let's check.** Have a volunteer pour the rice into the other container. Ask: **Does it all fit? Is there room for more?**

Have children continue to fill containers with rice and compare the capacities of containers.

(**Helpful Hint**)

Use small containers, a quart or less, so that filled containers are not too heavy.

USE AFTER LESSON 18.2

OBJECTIVE Discover how many cups, pints, or quarts are needed to fill a container

More or Less
Variation 1

Repeat "More or Less." Vary the activity by using cup, pint, and quart containers and identifying them by name. Ask: **How many cups are in a pint? How many pints are in a quart? How many cups are in a quart?**

Then have children estimate and measure to see if other containers hold more or less than a cup, pint, or quart.

USE AFTER LESSON 18.3

OBJECTIVE Compare which container holds more, less, or the same as a liter

More or Less
Variation 2

Repeat "More or Less." Vary the activity by using a liter container and identifying it by name. Place a quart bottle beside a litter bottle and ask: **Which holds more, the quart bottle or the liter bottle?**

Then have children estimate and measure to see if other containers hold more, less, or the same amount as a liter.

Dress for Success

OBJECTIVES Relate temperature to weather outdoors; relate outside temperature to clothes worn

MANAGEMENT Individuals

TIME 15 minutes

MATERIALS
- Dress for Success (p. 192)
- Story Mat (p. 244)
- oaktag

Before the Activity

Copy a Story Mat (p. 244) for each child. Cut out two thermometer cards from oaktag. Color in the mercury to indicate cold and hot temperatures. Place them facedown on a table so children can choose one without seeing what it is.

Modeling the Activity

Have a volunteer turn over one of the cards. Say: **Read the thermometer. Is the temperature hot or cold?** After children answer, say: **We're going to draw a picture that shows what it is like outside when it is that temperature. There will be people in the picture. How should the people be dressed?**

Have a volunteer turn over one of the cards. Have the children draw their own scenes to go with the temperature on the thermometer.

Helpful Hint

If the children live in a climate that does not have extremely cold or extremely warm temperatures, you might want to spend some time discussing what people would wear in those climates.

NUMBER OF THE WEEK
Spotlight on 37

NUMBER SENSE

OBJECTIVE Use the number 37 to solve problems in many contexts

MANAGEMENT Individuals

TIME 15 minutes

MATERIALS
- Spotlight on 37 (p. 221)

Modeling the Activity

Show children the Spotlight on 37 sheet (p. 221). Say: **Today we will explore some different ways that you can use the number 37.** Read the first exercise. Say: **Circle groups of ten marbles.** Then ask: **How many tens? How many ones? How many marbles in all?**

Ask a volunteer to read the other exercises to the class. Tell children that they may use coins or draw the coins in Exercise 2. After each set of directions, give children time to complete the exercise before moving on to the next set of directions.

Ask volunteers to explain their answer for Exercise 4.

Answers

1. 3; 7; 37
2. 37¢
3. 37
4. No; *Answers may vary. Sample:* No month has more than 31 days.

Unit 8 Planner
Chapter 19

Use after . . .

LESSON 19.1

Twice as Nice
Variation

For each group:
- Blank Spinner, p. 276
- Caterpillar Gameboard, pp. 290–291
- 2 counters

LESSON 19.2

Fact Path
Cross-Curricular

For each group:
- Addition Facts Through 20, p. 230
- Maze Gameboard, pp. 296–297
- game piece for each player

LESSON 19.3

Frame 10

For each student:
- Frame 10, p. 193
- Ten Frame Workmat, pp. 286–287
- 6-Part Spinner, p. 279
- connecting cubes (9 red, 9 green)

LESSON 19.4

Fact Path
Variation

For each group:
- Addition Facts Through 20, p. 230
- Maze Gameboard, pp. 296–297
- game piece for each player

LESSON 19.5

Number Groups
Vocabulary

For each pair:
- Number Groups, p. 194
- 40 connecting cubes

LESSON 19.6

Three in a Row
Variation

For each student:
- Three in a Row, p. 183
- 4-Part Spinner, p. 278
- crayons

LESSON 19.7

Number of the Week
Spotlight on 18

For each student:
- Spotlight on 18, p. 222

Chapter 19

USE AFTER LESSON 19.1

OBJECTIVE To solve doubles plus one facts for sums through 20

Twice as Nice
Variation

Repeat "Twice as Nice," following the directions on page 38. Create an answer sheet for doubles plus one to 20.

Use Number Cards 1–9 (p. 262) instead of the spinner. Have children identify the number on the card picked and then the sum of its double plus one.

So that the game does not end too quickly, have children move the number of spaces as shown on the number card, not the double plus one sum.

USE AFTER LESSON 19.2

CROSS-CURRICULAR
Science

OBJECTIVE Use 10 as an addend for sums through 20

MANAGEMENT Groups

TIME 15 minutes

MATERIALS PER GROUP
- Addition Facts Through 20 (p. 230)
- Maze Gameboard (pp. 296–297)
- game piece for each player

Fact Path

Before the Activity

Copy Addition Facts Through 20 (p. 230). Separate out the cards that have ten as an addend.

Modeling the Activity

Display the Maze Gameboard (pp. 296–297). Say: **We are going to play a game called *Race to the Moon*. The object of the game is to get to the moon first.** To help make the connection to science, ask the children to tell what they know about space travel.

Explain: **To start the game, we mix the playing cards. We put our game pieces on *Start*.** Mix the cards together and put them in a stack. Demonstrate with the card on the top of the pile. Say: **When it is your turn, take one card from the top of the pile. Read the addition problem aloud and tell the sum.**

Say: **The other players check your answer. Is my sum correct?** Let children check your answer. Say: **If the sum is greater than ten, I move five spaces. If the sum is ten or less, I move three spaces.** Demonstrate moving a game piece. You may want to show two or three different game paths you can take. Point out that the first person to get to *Finish* has arrived on the moon.

Frame 10

OBJECTIVE To make a 10 to add

MANAGEMENT Individuals

TIME 10 minutes

MATERIALS

- Frame 10 (p. 193)
- Ten Frame Workmat (pp. 286–287)
- 6-Part Spinners (p. 279)
- 18 connecting cubes, 9 each of red and green

Before the Activity

Label two 6-Part Spinners (p. 279), one 7, 7, 8, 8, 9, 9 and the other 4, 5, 6, 7, 8, 9.

Modeling the Activity

Display the spinners and tell children: **I am going to use these spinners to play an addition game.** Demonstrate as you say: **First I'll spin the 7–9 spinner. What number did I spin? I'll put that many red cubes on the Ten Frame Workmat** (pp. 286–287). Put red connecting cubes on the top ten frame on the Ten Frame Workmat, one to a square, starting at the top left and going left to right. Say: **Now I'll spin the 4–9 spinner and put that many green cubes on the mat.** Put green connecting cubes on the Ten Frame Workmat, beginning in the next square after the last red cube. Fill the bottom ten frame when the top ten frame is full.

Then ask: **Now how many cubes do I have in all? How do the ten frames on the mat help me to find the sum?**

Children can repeat the activity independently.

Fact Path
Variation

OBJECTIVE Use strategies to practice addition facts through 12

Repeat "Fact Path," as described on page 118. Vary the activity by using all the addition facts to 12. Use the same gameboard, but call it *The Maze* rather than *Race to the Moon.*

This time have children name the strategy they might use to find the answer. For example, ask: **Will you use part-part-whole, doubles, or a ten frame to help you find the answer?**

Number Groups

Modeling the Activity

VOCABULARY

OBJECTIVE Discover other names for numbers

MANAGEMENT Pairs

TIME 15 minutes

MATERIALS PER PAIR
• Number Groups (p. 194)

• 40 connecting cubes

Introduce the activity. Say: **We can find different names for one number. Choose any number from 11 to 18.** Let a volunteer choose one number. Demonstrate on a sheet of paper as you explain: **I'm going to write that number at the top of the page. Now we will count out that number of cubes.** Have another volunteer put the cubes into a single group, one at a time, while the rest of the children help count.

Say: **We can find other names for this number by dividing the cubes into two groups. How many cubes should we put in one group? How many cubes will we have left for the other group?** Separate the cubes into two groups, according to children's suggestion. Then say: **Now we have a new name for the number we started with. We can write that name as an addition sentence.** Write the addition sentence below the number. Ask: **Do you think we can find another name for the number?**

Repeat this process, dividing the cubes into two different groups to make as many number sentences as possible. Write the new addition sentences below the first one.

Helpful Hint

Partners take turns. One child divides the cubes into groups, and the other child writes the addition sentence.

Three in a Row
Variation

OBJECTIVE Find the sum of three numbers

Repeat "Three in a Row," as described on page 100. Vary the activity by preparing a 6-Part Spinner (p. 279) labeled 1–6. Ask: **Did you use doubles, make a 10, or add in any order when you added the three numbers?**

NUMBER OF THE WEEK
Spotlight on 18

NUMBER SENSE

OBJECTIVE Use the
number 18 to solve
problems in many contexts

MANAGEMENT Individuals

TIME 15 minutes

MATERIALS
• Spotlight on 18 (p. 222)

Modeling the Activity

Show children the Spotlight on 18 sheet (p. 222). Say: **Today
we will explore some different ways that you can use the
number 18.** Read the first exercise. Ask the children whether
the pole or the stick is longer. Then have them circle their
choice.

Ask a volunteer to read the other exercises to the class. After
each set of directions, give children time to complete the
exercise before moving on to the next set of directions.

Discuss with children how they know that there are more
cubes than spheres in Exercise 4. Some children might count
cubes and spheres and then compare. Others might draw
lines matching a cube to a sphere.

Answers

1. pole

2. 18

3. 18 children

4. cubes; *Answer may vary. Sample:* I counted the cubes and
the spheres and compared the numbers.

Unit 8 Planner
Chapter 20

Use after . . .

LESSON 20.1

Double Spin

For each student:
- Double Spin, p. 195
- Blank Spinner, p. 276
- Addition/Subtraction Sentences, p. 231
- counters

LESSON 20.2

Subtraction Cubes

For each pair:
- Subtraction Cubes, p. 196
- Addition Facts Through 20, p. 230
- Addition/Subtraction Sentences, p. 231
- connecting cubes (14 cubes each of two colors)

LESSON 20.3

Subtraction Cubes
Variation 1

For each pair:
- Subtraction Cubes, p. 196
- Addition Facts Through 20, p. 230
- Addition/Subtraction Sentences, p. 231
- connecting cubes (14 cubes each of two colors)

LESSON 20.4

Subtraction Cubes
Variation 2

For each pair:
- Subtraction Cubes, p. 196
- Addition Facts Through 20, p. 230
- Addition/Subtraction Sentences, p. 231
- connecting cubes (14 cubes each of two colors)

LESSON 20.5

Missing Numbers

For each pair:
- Missing Numbers, p. 197
- Part-Part-Whole Workmat, pp. 284–285
- index cards
- 20 two-sided counters

LESSON 20.6

Family Fun
Variation

For each pair:
- Family Fun, p. 156
- Number Cards 1–9, +, −, =, pp. 262–263, 267

LESSON 20.7

Number of the Week Spotlight on 15

For each student:
- Spotlight on 15, p. 223

Chapter 20

USE AFTER LESSON 20.1

OBJECTIVE Use doubles to subtract

MANAGEMENT Individuals

TIME 15 minutes

MATERIALS
- Double Spin (p. 195)
- Blank Spinner (p. 276)
- Addition/Subtraction Sentences (p. 231)
- counters

Double Spin

Before the Activity

Make an 8-section Spinner (p. 276). Label as follows: *6, 8, 10, 12, 14, 16, 18,* and *20.* Copy Addition/Subtraction Sentences (p. 231) and count out 20 counters for each pair.

Modeling the Activity

Display the spinner. Ask: **Are the numbers on the spinner even or odd?** Remind children that if they can show a number in pairs with no leftovers, then the number is even.

Choose two volunteers to demonstrate using a doubles fact to subtract. Have one child spin. Say: **Count out that number of counters. Place them in two equal rows.** Help the child write an addition sentence. Ask: **How many counters are in the top row? Write the number on the first line. Now write a plus sign in the circle.** Repeat with the bottom row and have the child write an equal sign in the circle. Then have the child find the sum. Ask: **Is this a doubles fact? How do you know?** Now have the partner use the doubles fact to write a subtraction sentence. Ask: **How many counters do you have in all? Write the number.** Then say: **Take away the bottom row. Write how many you took away.** Now say: **Count how many counters you have left. Write the difference.**

Ask: **How do you know that [4 + 4 = 8] and [8 − 4 = 4] are related?** Pairs take turns and continue the activity.

(**Helpful Hint**)

To guide children in setting counters in two equal rows, you might suggest that they put the counters in pairs.

Subtraction Cubes

OBJECTIVE Subtract from 13 and 14 by using related addition facts

MANAGEMENT Pairs

TIME 15 minutes

MATERIALS PER PAIR
- Subtraction Cubes (p. 196)
- Addition Facts Through 20 (p. 230)
- Addition/Subtraction Sentences (p. 231)
- connecting cubes (14 cubes each of two colors)

Before the Activity

Copy Addition Facts Through 20 (p. 230). Prepare cards with facts for 13 and 14. Display Addition/Subtraction Sentences (p. 231). Complete the two addition sentences. Show the fact cards and cubes that reflect the sentences.

Modeling the Activity

Focus attention on the cubes. Review the complete sentences. Point to each number as you say: **Count the [blue] cubes. Count the [green] cubes. Count how many in all.** Have a volunteer complete the subtraction sentences in the same way. Then say: **How do you know this is a fact family?** Remind children that all the facts in a family use the same three numbers.

Have children play in pairs. One child turns over the top card and reads the addition aloud. Say: **Show the fact with cubes. Write the addition.** Pause and say: **Now write another addition fact in the family.** Then have the partner model and write two subtraction sentences in the fact family. Ask: **Why are these part of the same fact family?**

Partners take turns turning over a card, showing the addition, and showing the subtraction.

Subtraction Cubes
Variation 1

OBJECTIVE Subtract from 15 and 16 using related addition facts

Before the Activity

Repeat "Subtraction Cubes" as described in Lesson 20.2. Vary the activity by using Addition Fact cards for 15 and 16.

Modeling the Activity

Play "Subtraction Cubes." Have children play the activity in the same way but use the addition facts for 15 and 16. Say: **You will model and write related addition and subtraction facts.** Give pairs 16 cubes of one color and 16 cubes of another color.

USE AFTER LESSON 20.4

OBJECTIVE Subtract from 17 through 20 using related addition facts

Subtraction Cubes
Variation 2

Before the Activity

Repeat "Subtraction Cubes" as described in Lesson 20.2. Vary the activity by using Addition Fact cards for 17 through 20.

Modeling the Activity

Play "Subtraction Cubes," following the directions on page 124. Have children play the activity in the same way but use the addition facts for 17 through 20. Say: **You will model and write related addition and subtraction facts.** Give pairs 20 cubes of one color and 20 cubes of another color.

USE AFTER LESSON 20.5

OBJECTIVE Find the missing addend and difference in related facts

MANAGEMENT Pairs

TIME 15 minutes

MATERIALS PER PAIR
- Missing Numbers (p. 197)
- Part-Part-Whole Workmat (pp. 284–285)
- index cards
- 20 two-sided counters

Missing Numbers

Before the Activity

Prepare sets of index cards with related facts. The addition fact has a missing addend. The subtraction fact is missing the difference. Copy a Part-Part-Whole Workmat (pp. 284–285).

Modeling the Activity

Discuss with children when they might use subtraction in their lives. For example, baking 6 muffins and eating 1. Place the cards facedown in pairs. Have children use the Part-Part-Whole Workmat and counters to find missing numbers. Call on volunteers to demonstrate. Turn over a pair of cards and say: **Look at the subtraction sentence. Can you find the difference?** Ask: **What is the whole?** Place that many counters in the whole section of the mat. Then ask: **How many are you taking away?** Guide the child to move that many counters to the part section. Ask: **So what is the difference?** Say the complete subtraction sentence.

Have the partner use the related subtraction fact to find the missing addend. Remind children that related addition and subtraction facts use the same three numbers. Say: **Look at the addition. You know how many in all. You know one part. How can you use the subtraction fact to help you find the missing part?** Help children understand that they can use the two parts in the subtraction fact to help them find the missing addend.

Pairs take turns completing the related facts. Encourage them to model each fact with counters and the workmat.

**USE AFTER
LESSON 20.6**

Family Fun
Variation

OBJECTIVE Complete a family of facts

Before the Activity

Repeat "Family Fun" as described in Lesson 6.5. Vary the activity by using Number Cards 0–20 (pp. 262–264) and $+$, $-$, and $=$ symbol cards.

Modeling the Activity

Play "Family Fun," following the directions on page 45. Play the same activity, but have children show addition facts through 20.

**USE AFTER
LESSON 20.7**

NUMBER OF THE WEEK
Spotlight on 15

NUMBER SENSE

OBJECTIVE Use the number 15 to solve problems in many contexts

MANAGEMENT Individuals

TIME 15 minutes

MATERIALS
• Spotlight on 15 (p. 223)

Before the Activity

Make a copy of Spotlight on 15 (p. 223) for each child.

Modeling the Activity

Show children the Spotlight on 15 sheet. Say: **Today we will explore different ways to use the number 15.** Read the first activity. Ask: **How many groups of 5 are in 15?** Have a volunteer demonstrate making groups of 5.

Ask a volunteer to read the other exercises to the class. After each set of directions, give children time to complete the exercise before moving on to the next set of directions.

Answers

1. 5 groups

2. $7 + 8 = 15$; $8 + 7 = 15$; $15 - 7 = 8$; $15 - 8 = 7$

3. Beth, 2 more

4. 5, 10, 15, 20, 25, 30, 35; Answers may vary.

Unit 8 Planner
Chapter 21

Use after . . .

Copyright © Houghton Mifflin Company. All Rights Reserved.

LESSON 21.1
Tens and Tens

For each pair:
- Tens and Tens, p. 198
- 9 tens blocks
- 90 connecting cubes

LESSON 21.2
Roll into Place

For each pair:
- Roll into Place, p. 199
- Tens and Ones Workmat, pp. 288–289
- 4-Part Spinner, p. 278
- number cube
- place-value blocks (6 tens and 8 ones)

LESSON 21.3
Pick and Spin
Cross-Curricular

For each student:
- Pick and Spin, p. 200
- 4-Part Spinner, p. 278
- Number Cards 20–44, pp. 264–266
- Tens and Ones Workmat, pp. 288–289
- Place-Value Sheet, p. 243
- 9 tens blocks, 9 ones blocks

LESSON 21.4
Pick and Spin
Variation

For each student:
- Pick and Spin, p. 200
- 4-Part Spinner, p. 278
- Number Cards 20–44, pp. 264–266
- Tens and Ones Workmat, pp. 288–289
- Place-Value Sheet, p. 243
- 9 tens blocks, 9 ones blocks

LESSON 21.5
Roll into Place
Variation

For each pair:
- Roll into Place, p. 199
- Tens and Ones Workmat, pp. 288–289
- 4-Part Spinner, p. 278
- number cube
- place-value blocks (6 tens and 8 ones)

LESSON 21.6
**Number of the Week
Spotlight on 49**

For each student:
- Spotlight on 49, p. 224

Chapter 21

OBJECTIVE Add multiples of 10 and recognize a pattern

MANAGEMENT Pairs

TIME 15 minutes

MATERIALS PER PAIR
- Tens and Tens (p. 198)
- 9 tens blocks
- 90 connecting cubes

Tens and Tens

Modeling the Activity

Display 9 tens blocks on a table. Say: **Each block is "ten" because each block is made of ten ones blocks.** Count aloud to verify that each tens block is made up of ten ones blocks.

Call on two volunteers to demonstrate. Say: **Each of you pick some tens.** Ask each child: **How many tens did you pick? What is your number?**

Then have children combine their tens blocks. Ask: **Now how many tens do you have altogether? What is the sum?** Have children explain how they arrived at their answers.

Explain that partners will take turns picking the first group of tens.

At the end of the activity, ask: **How does knowing how many tens help you find the sum?**

> **Helpful Hint**

Explain that children don't have to pick all 9 tens blocks each turn.

OBJECTIVE Use place-value blocks to represent 1-digit and 2-digit addition problems without regrouping

MANAGEMENT Pairs

TIME 10 minutes

MATERIALS PER PAIR
- Roll into Place (p. 199)
- Tens and Ones Workmat (pp. 288–289)
- 4-Part Spinner (p. 278)
- number cube
- 6 tens and 8 ones place-value blocks

Roll into Place

Before the Activity

Label the number cube with numbers 1 to 6 and the 4-Part Spinner with numbers 1, 2, 3, 4.

Modeling the Activity

Display the Tens and Ones Workmat (pp. 288–289) and the place-value blocks. Say: **We can use the blocks and the mat to add greater numbers.** Let a volunteer roll the number cube. Ask: **What number does the cube show? We will use the number cube to show tens. How many tens blocks will we put in the tens place?** Have children count along as the volunteer puts that many tens blocks in the tens column. Let the volunteer spin the spinner. Ask: **What number does the spinner show? That's how many ones blocks we will put in the ones place.** Encourage children to count along as the volunteer puts that many ones blocks in the ones column. Ask: **What number have we made?**

Say: **Now we will spin the spinner again to find another number.** Let a volunteer spin the spinner. Ask: **What number does the spinner show? That is how many blocks we will add to the ones place.** Have the volunteer put that many ones blocks below those already in the ones column. Be sure to leave a space between the two sets of cubes in the ones column. Ask: **What number have we made?**

Say: **Now let's add the two numbers. How many ones?** Let children count along as you point to each block in the ones column. **How many tens?** Let the children count along as you point to each block in the tens column.

Say: **What is the sum?** Confirm, saying, for example: **Yes, 32 + 4 = 36.** Discuss places where the children might be adding a 1-digit and a 2-digit number.

You may want to repeat the process before letting children complete the activity independently.

**USE AFTER
LESSON 21.3**

CROSS-CURRICULAR
Social Studies

OBJECTIVE Use place-value blocks to add two 2-digit numbers without regrouping

MANAGEMENT Individuals

TIME 15 minutes

MATERIALS PER PAIR

- Pick and Spin (p. 200)

- 4-Part Spinner (p. 278)

- Number Cards 20–44 (pp. 264–266)

- Tens and Ones Workmat (pp. 288–289)

- Place Value Recording Sheet (p. 243)

- 9 tens blocks, 9 ones blocks

Pick and Spin

Before the Activity

Divide the 4-Part Spinner (p. 278) into sections: 11, 22, 33, 44. Photocopy and cut the 2-digit Number Cards. Use only cards 20, 22, 24, 31, 33, 35, 40, and 44. Prepare the Tens and Ones Workmat (pp. 288–289).

Modeling the Activity

Say: **Today we are going to pretend we are farmers counting and packing tomatoes. We will pack our tomatoes in boxes of ten.**

Display the Number Cards and the spinner. Explain: **We are going to use these Number Cards and the spinner to practice adding greater numbers.**

Place the Number Cards facedown in a pile. A volunteer picks one card and reads the number aloud. Say: **Use blocks to show the number on the Number Card. This shows the number of tomatoes.** Guide the volunteer in counting out tens and ones blocks to match the number on the card. Place the blocks in the appropriate columns on the Tens and Ones Workmat.

Ask the volunteer to find another number by spinning the spinner. Ask: **What number did you spin?** Then say: **Now put out more blocks to show the number on the spinner.** Make sure the volunteer places the second set of blocks below the first set in each column of the work mat.

Say: **We are going to add. Which do we add first, the tens or the ones?** After children answer, help them count the ones. Say: **I'll write that number in the ones column.** Write the number in the ones column of the Place Value Recording Sheet. Repeat, adding and recording the tens. Ask: **How many boxes of tomatoes do we have? How many single tomatoes do we have?** Children repeat the activity independently, using all the Number Cards.

USE AFTER LESSON 21.4

OBJECTIVE Use different ways to add

Pick and Spin
Variation

Repeat "Pick and Spin," following the directions on page 129. Vary the activity by changing the spinner to 3, 20, 34, and 2, and using cards 21, 22, 24, 31, 35, 40, and 44. Tell children that in this activity they are going to pretend that they work for a company that makes pencils. They are packing ten pencils to a box. For each addition problem, have the children decide if they will use mental math, pencil and paper, or place-value blocks to find the sum. Then have them work the problem. Tell the children that there may be many ways to solve the problem and no one way is best. The strategy they use for a problem will depend on the numbers.

USE AFTER LESSON 21.5

CROSS-CURRICULAR
Social Studies

OBJECTIVE Practice adding two 2-digit numbers without regrouping

Roll into Place
Variation

Repeat "Roll into Place" as described on page 128. Vary the activity by changing the numbers on the number cube to 1, 2, 3, 4, 4, and 5.

Say: **When we travel, we need to keep track of our miles. We are going to use the numbers on the number cube and spinner to list the miles we travel in the morning and in the afternoon. We will then add the two numbers to find how many miles we traveled during the day.** Have children make two 2-digit numbers in the same manner they made the first 2-digit number in "Roll into Place." Have the children record the problem on a sheet of paper.

Children repeat the activity independently three more times. Then on a state or city map, point out how far some of the distances they found are from the state's capital or their own city or town.

NUMBER OF THE WEEK
Spotlight on 49

NUMBER SENSE

OBJECTIVE Use the number 49 to solve problems in many contexts.

MANAGEMENT Individuals

TIME 15 minutes

MATERIALS
• Spotlight on 49 (p. 224)

Modeling the Activity

Show children Spotlight on 49 (p. 224). Say: **Today we will explore some different ways that you can use the number 49.** Read the first exercise. Ask the children what number comes just before 49 and what number comes just after 49. Have them write their answers in the spaces on the Spotlight on 49 sheet.

Ask a volunteer to read the other exercises to the class. After each set of directions, give children time to complete the exercise before moving on to the next set of directions.

Ask volunteers to talk about Exercise 4 and whether they could use mental math to add 40 + 9. Accept reasonable answers. Some children will feel confident to do the problem in their head. Others will feel they need to write the problem down.

Answers

1. 48, 50

2. turn

3. can of vegetables

4. *Answers may vary. Sample:* Yes. 9 is close to 10. 10 + 40 = 50. 40 + 9 = 49.

Unit 8 Planner
Chapter 22

Use after . . .

LESSON 22.1	**LESSON 22.2**	**LESSON 22.3**	**LESSON 22.4**
Take It Away	**Rolling Away**	**Number Boxes**	**Rolling Away** *Variation*
For each pair: • Playing Card Master, p. 274 • number cube • tens blocks	For each pair: • Rolling Away, p. 201 • 6-Part Spinner, p. 279 • number cube • place-value blocks	For each student: • Number Boxes, p. 202 • Number Cards 1–50, pp. 262–267 • Tens and Ones Workmat, pp. 288–289 • 2 small boxes • 4 tens blocks, 9 ones blocks	For each pair: • Rolling Away, p. 201 • 6-Part Spinner, p. 279 • number cube • place-value blocks

LESSON 22.5	**LESSON 22.6**	**LESSON 22.7**	
Spin Away *Cross-Curricular*	**Apart and Together**	**Number of the Week Spotlight on 36**	
For each student: • Spin Away, p. 203 • 6-Part Spinner, p. 279 (two) • 5 tens blocks and 9 ones blocks	For each pair: • Number Cards 45–59, pp. 267–268 • 10-Part Spinner, p. 280 • Part-Part-Whole Workmat, pp. 284–285 • 60 counters	For each student: • Spotlight on 36, p. 225	

Chapter 22

USE AFTER LESSON 22.1

OBJECTIVE Subtract tens

MANAGEMENT Pairs

TIME 15 minutes

MATERIALS PER PAIR
- Playing Card Master (p. 274)
- number cube
- tens blocks

Take It Away

Before the Activity

Use Playing Card Master (p. 274) to make 2 sets of cards as follows: 10, 20, 30, 40, and 50. Label a number cube 90, 90, 80, 80, 70, 60. Display the tens blocks.

Modeling the Activity

Place the number cards facedown in a pile. Ask a volunteer to roll the number cube and say the number aloud. [80]
Ask: **How many tens are in this number?** Have the child group [8] tens blocks together. Remind children that 80 is another way to write 8 tens.

Now have another volunteer turn over the top card [50] and read the number aloud. Tell the pair they will now subtract [50] from [80]. Ask: **How many tens are in [50]?** Have the child take away [5] tens blocks. Then ask: **How many tens blocks are left? [3] So 8 tens minus 5 tens is 3 tens. What is 80 minus 50?** [30]

Have children take turns rolling the cube, turning over a card, and telling their partner the difference.

> **Helpful Hint**
>
> You might want to use models to emphasize place value in comparing two numbers such as 5 and 50.

USE AFTER LESSON 22.2

OBJECTIVE Subtract 1-digit numbers without regrouping

MANAGEMENT Pairs

TIME 10 minutes

MATERIALS PER PAIR
- Rolling Away (p. 201)
- 6-Part Spinner (p. 279)
- number cube
- place-value blocks

Rolling Away

Before the Activity

Prepare the number cube with the following labels: 27, 28, 38, 39, 46, 47. Label the 6-Part Spinner (p. 279) sections as follows: 1, 2, 3, 4, 5, 6.

Modeling the Activity

Display the number cube and the place-value blocks. Have a volunteer roll the cube and say the number. Say: **Show the number with blocks. How many tens? How many ones?** Let children count along as the volunteer displays the correct number of blocks.

Now have the child spin the spinner to find a number to subtract. [2] Then say: **Take away [2] ones blocks.** Again, have children count along. Ask: **What is the difference?**

Choose another volunteer. Have him or her say the subtraction problem. Then say: **Write the subtraction problem.** Guide the child to write the subtraction problem vertically on a sheet of paper. Remind children to carefully align the ones as they write the subtraction problem.

USE AFTER LESSON 22.3

Number Boxes

OBJECTIVE Subtract 2-digit numbers without regrouping

MANAGEMENT Individuals

TIME 15 minutes

MATERIALS
- Number Boxes (p. 202)
- Number Cards 1–50 (pp. 262–267)
- Tens and Ones Workmat (pp. 288–289)
- 2 small boxes
- 4 tens blocks, 9 ones blocks

Before the Activity

Label two small boxes Box A and Box B. Place Number Cards 25–29, 35–39, and 45–49 (pp. 264–267) facedown in Box A. Place Number Cards 1–4, 10–14, 20–24 (pp. 262–264) facedown in Box B.

Modeling the Activity

Display the Tens and Ones Workmat (pp. 288–289) and the place-value blocks. Review the difference between the ones place and the tens place on the mat. Tell children they will use the blocks and mat to model subtraction. Have a volunteer take a card from Box A and read the number aloud. [37] Say: **Count tens and ones blocks aloud to show the number. Place them on the mat.**

Have the child take a number from Box B. [11] Say: **This is the number you will subtract.** Remind children to subtract the ones first. Say: **How many ones are in [11]? How many ones blocks will you take away from [37]?** Have children count along as the child removes the correct number of ones blocks from the workmat. Repeat with tens.

Then guide the child to write the subtraction in vertical form. Say: **What number did you start with? What number did you take away? What is the difference?**

Have children work independently to continue picking cards, modeling, and writing the subtraction.

USE AFTER LESSON 22.4

Rolling Away
Variation

OBJECTIVE Choose ways to subtract 2-digit numbers

Repeat "Rolling Away," following the directions on page 133. Label a number cube with numbers 45, 57, 59, 68, 76, 85, and label the 6-Part Spinner (p. 279) with numbers 2, 10, 24, 30, 31, 35. Children decide how they will subtract before doing it.

Ask: **What way will you use to subtract? Will you use mental math, paper and pencil, or blocks?** Allow children time to decide what way they think is best. Then say: **Tell why you chose that way.**

USE AFTER LESSON 22.5

CROSS-CURRICULUM
Language Arts

OBJECTIVE Practice 2-digit subtraction without regrouping

MANAGEMENT Individuals

TIME 15 minutes

MATERIALS
- Spin Away (p. 203)
- Two 6-Part Spinners (p. 279)
- 5 tens blocks and 9 ones blocks

Spin Away

Before the Activity

Label one spinner (p. 279) with numbers 27, 28, 25, 39, 46, 57; label the other spinner 2, 3, 5, 12, 13, 15.

Modeling the Activity

Display the spinners and the place-value blocks. Say: **We can begin a subtraction problem by spinning a number on the 27 to 57 spinner.** Have a volunteer spin it. Ask: **What number did you spin? Show that number with blocks.** Have children count along as the volunteer displays the correct number of tens and ones blocks.

Say: **Now we'll roll the red cube to choose a number to subtract. This time we'll use the 2 to 15 spinner.** Have children count as the volunteer removes that many blocks. Ask: **What is the difference?**

Then guide children in stating the subtraction problem. Say: **We can write a subtraction problem to show the two numbers and the difference.** Write the subtraction problem vertically on the board.

After children have created several subtraction sentences, have them pick one and write a story about the numbers.

Helpful Hints

1. Be sure children spin the 27 to 57 spinner first.
2. Remind children to remove the ones blocks first.

USE AFTER LESSON 22.6

OBJECTIVES See how addition and subtraction are related; write number sentences for addition and subtraction

MANAGEMENT Pairs

TIME 15 minutes

MATERIALS PER PAIR
- Number Cards 45–59 (pp. 267–268)
- 10-Part Spinner (p. 280)
- Part-Part-Whole Workmat (pp. 284–285)
- 60 counters

Apart and Together

Before the Activity

Copy Number Cards (pp. 267–268). Cut out and separate 45–49 and 55–59. Label a 10-Part Spinner (p. 280) 30–34 and 40–44.

Modeling the Activity

Place the cards facedown on the table with the Part-Part-Whole Workmat (pp. 284–285). Say: **First we'll pick a card from the top of the deck. That card tells us how many counters to place in the *whole* section of the mat.** Say: **Since the card shows 56, I'll put 56 counters in the *whole* section of the mat.** Have children count aloud as you place the counters on the mat. Then spin the spinner. Say: **The spinner shows 31 so I'll move 31 counters from the *whole* section into one *part* section of the workmat.** Have children count aloud as you move the counters. Say: **I'll move the rest of the** counters into the other *part* section as you count them aloud. Help children write a subtraction sentence to express the operation, such as 56 − 31 = 25.

Next say: **Now we'll put the two parts back together.** Have children count as you move the counters from each *part* section back into the *whole* section of the workmat. Then have them write an addition sentence to express the operation, such as 31 + 25 = 56.

Children take turns placing the counters and writing the number sentence.

USE AFTER LESSON 22.7

Number of the Week
Spotlight on 36

NUMBER SENSE

OBJECTIVE Use the number 36 to solve problems in many contexts

MANAGEMENT Individuals

TIME 15 minutes

MATERIALS
• Spotlight on 36 (p. 225)

Modeling the Activity

Show children the Spotlight on 36 sheet (p. 225). Say: **Today we will explore some different ways that you can use the number 36.** Read the first exercise. Ask the children to circle the number they think is *even*.

Ask a volunteer to read the other exercises to the class. After each set of directions, give children time to complete the exercise before moving on to the next set of directions.

Allow time for volunteers to talk about Exercise 4 and how they know that the answer is *cold*.

Answers

1. 36

2. 6

3.

4. cold; *Answers may vary. Sample:* The thermometer is low; the child is in a big coat.

Towers Up

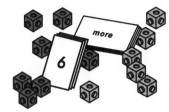

1. Choose a blue tower.

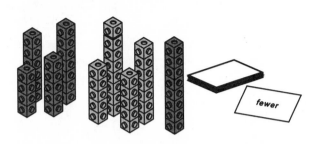

2. Show your partner. Choose a card. Read the card.

3. Your partner finds a yellow tower to match the card.

4. Keep playing. Take turns.

 **Try This!**

Pick a handful of cubes.
Count the cubes.
Pick a card. Count cubes to match the word on the card.

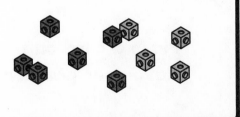

Dot-to-Dot

What You'll Need:

1. Pass out all the cards.

2. Place cards on the table. Place all matching cards in a pile.

3. Cover your eyes. Choose a card. Find a match.

4. Keep playing. Match all your cards.

Try This!

Place a card on the table.
Have your partner match it.

Activities

Chairs

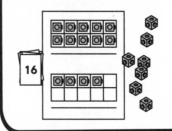

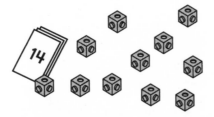

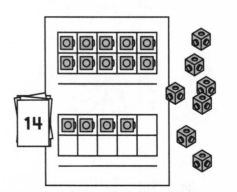

1. Choose a number card. Read the number. Tell a number story.

2. Your partner puts cubes on the ten frame.

Activities

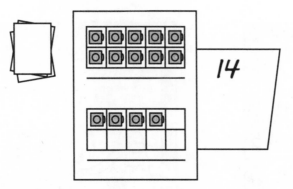

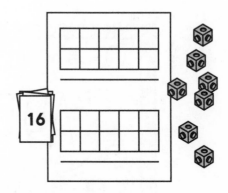

3. Count to check. Write the number.

4. Switch roles. Keep playing.

Try This!

Take a handful of cubes.
Count them.
Find the number card to
match the number of cubes.

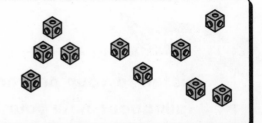

Draw and Tell

What You'll Need:

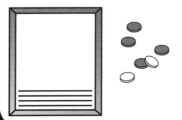

1. Make up a story.
Draw where it happens.

2. Use counters.
Act it out.

3. Tell how many in all.

Try This!

Listen to your partner's story.
Talk about how your stories are different.

Activities

Shake and Spill

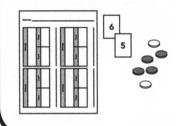

1. Pick a number card.

2. Put that many counters in the cup.

3. Shake and spill. Find the parts.

Whole		Whole	
6			
Part	**Part**	**Part**	**Part**
●●●	○○		

Whole		Whole	
Part	**Part**	**Part**	**Part**

Name:

4. Try again.

Try This!

Play again. Put 4 counters in the cup.

Sum It Up

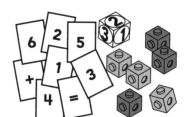

1. Roll the number cube. Build that many yellow cubes.

 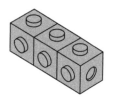

2. Let your partner roll. Build that many blue cubes.

3. How many cubes in all? Show the number sentence.

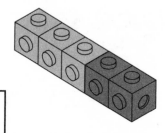

| 3 | + | 2 | = | 5 |

4. Play the game two more times. Show the number sentences.

Try This!

Draw a picture to show 3 + 3 = 6.

Activities

Just the Same

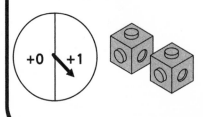

1. Use three cubes.
Make a train.

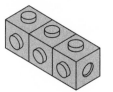
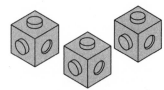

2. Spin.
Do what the spinner says.

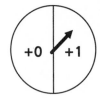
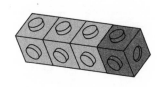

3. Take turns.
Each player gets three turns.

4. Count how many cubes you have now.

Try This!

Write an addition sentence for your last spin.

Activities

Missing Part Stories

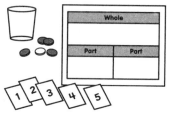

1. Put 5 counters in the cup.
Pick a number card.

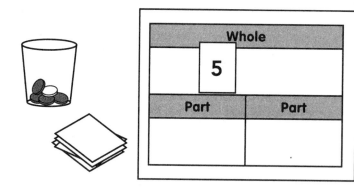

2. Your partner takes out that many counters.

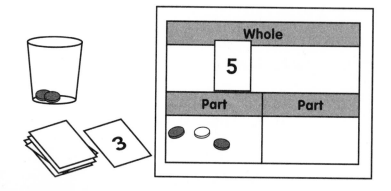

3. Tell how many counters are left in the cup.

4. Take turns. Keep going until you both have had three turns.

Try This!

Tell stories for 4 apples.
Use number cards 1, 2, and 3.

Count and Take Away

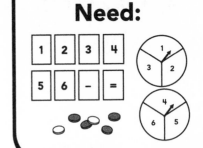
1. Spin the 4–6 Spinner.
Put out that many counters.

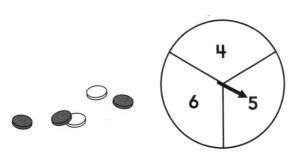

2. Your partner spins the 1–3 Spinner.
Take away that many counters.

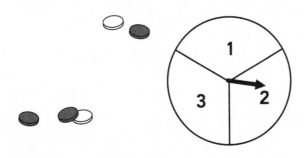

3. How many are left?
Make a subtraction sentence.

| 5 | – | 2 | = | 3 |

 Try This!

Use 6 counters.
Let your partner take some away.
How many are left?

Activities

Picture This!

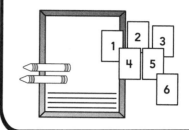

6

1. Put out the 6 card.

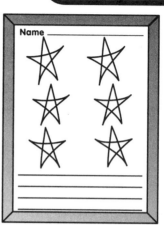

2. Draw 6 stars.

2

3. Pick another card.

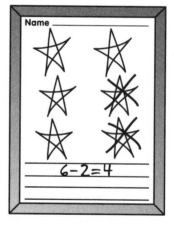

6−2=4

4. Subtract that many stars. Write the subtraction sentence.

Try This!

Look at this picture.
Write the number sentence.

Take Some Away

1. Draw a picture.

2. Make up a subtraction number story.

3. Your partner crosses things out.
Write the subtraction sentence two ways.

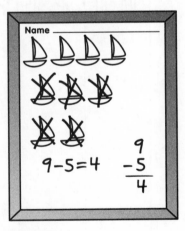

$9 - 5 = 4$

$$\begin{array}{r} 9 \\ -5 \\ \hline 4 \end{array}$$

Try This!

Look at the picture.
Write the number sentence
two ways.

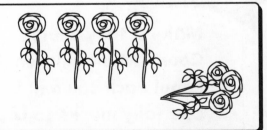

Activities

Tally Ho!

1. Count the cubes.

2. Count one cube at a time. Record each cube with a tally mark.

3. Count the tally marks. Write how many.

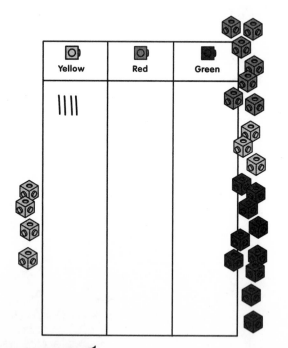

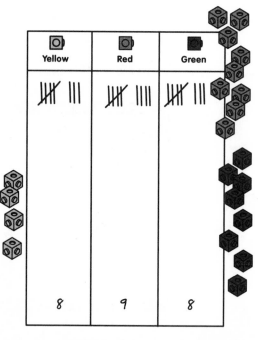

Try This!

Make a tally chart.
Count what children have on their feet.
Label each column: Sneakers, Shoes, Sandals.
Use tally marks to count.

Get the Picture?

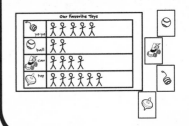
1. Look at the graph.
Talk about it.

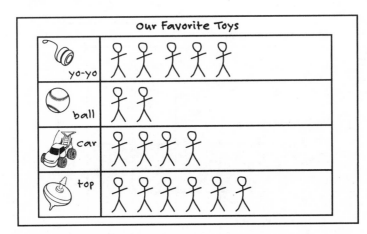

2. Turn over 2 cards.

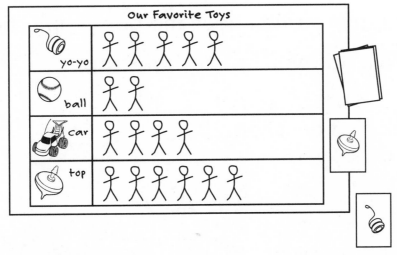

3. Use the cards. Ask your partner a question.

Try This!

2 more children choose a car.
How many cars are there in all?
How many more children chose
a car than a yo-yo?

Seasonal Bars

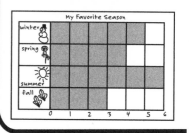

1. Look at the bar graph.
   Talk about it.

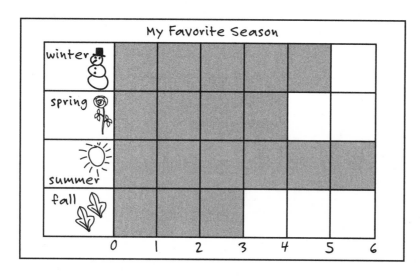

What information does the bar graph show?

2. Explain how you read a bar graph.

3. Use the graph.
   Think of a question.
   Ask a classmate.

How many children like spring best?

Try This!

How many children like spring and fall?
Write a number sentence.

Favorite Fruit Survey

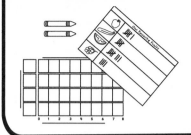

1. Look at the survey results.

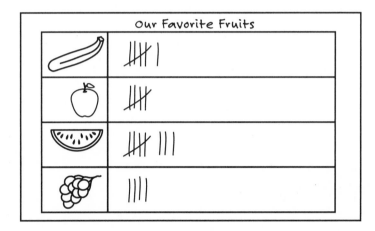

2. Use the bar graph.
Write the title.
Write the labels.

3. Use the tally chart.
Complete the bar
graph.

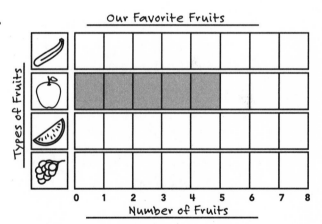

Use the information on the graph.
Ask a question.

Try This!

Ask your classmates a queston.
Make a tally chart of their answers.
Use the tally chart to make a graph.

Activities

How Many?

What You'll Need:

1. Pick a card.
Put that many counters in the cup.

Activities

2. Your partner puts more counters next to the cup.

3. Count on.
How many counters are there in all?

4. Try again.
Keep picking cards and taking turns.

Try This!

Write an addition to show one of your picks.

Line Up Facts

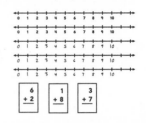

1. Pick 1 card.

$$\begin{array}{r} 3 \\ + 5 \\ \hline \end{array}$$

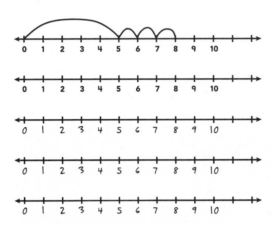

3 + 5 = 8

2. Use a number line.
Add the numbers.

3. Write the number
sentence.

4. Pick 3 more cards.
Find the sums.

Try This!

**Look at the number line.
Write the addition
sentence.**

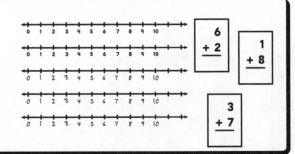

_____

Back Down

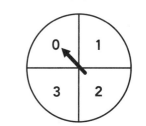

1. Write the
number
10.
Spin.

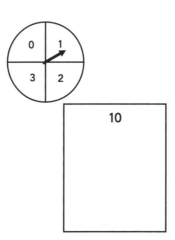

10

2. Count back that many.
Write the new number.

10
9

3. Spin again.
Count back from your
last number.

10
9
7

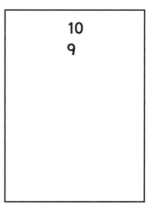

4. Keep going until you
reach zero or until you can't subtract.

Try This!

This time start with number 7.
Count back until you reach zero.

Activities

Along the Line

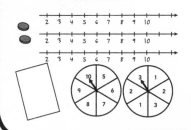

1. Spin the
5–10 spinner.

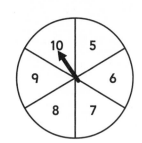

Place your counter above the number.

2. Spin the 1–3 spinner.
Move your counter
back.

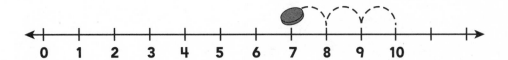

3. Write a subtraction sentence.

$$10 - 3 = 7$$

Try This!

Write two facts.
Give them to your partner to solve.
Use the number line.

Family Fun

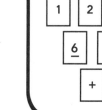
1. Turn over a number card. Your partner turns over a card too.

4	5

2. Put down a . Finish the fact.

4	+	5	=	9

3. Show the other fact with +.

5	+	4	=	9

4. Show the facts with −.

9	−	4	=	5
9	−	5	=	4

Choose more numbers.
Show the fact families for them.

Try This!

Make a number sentence.
Then take away one card.
Ask your partner what is missing.

Draw the Twin

1. Your partner looks away.
You make a shape.

2. Describe your shape.
Do not let your
partner see.
Have your partner
draw the shape.

3. Do the shapes
match?

4. Take turns.

Try This!

Call out the name of a shape. You can call out
triangle, rectangle, square, or circle.
Have your partner draw the shape.

Activities

Face to Face

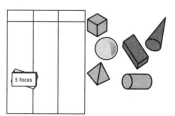

1. Pick three labels.
Place one in each column.
Look at the solid shapes.

12 edges	0 corners	5 faces

0 edges

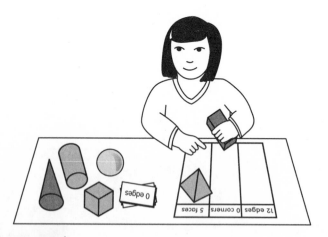

2. Sort solid shapes.

3. Pick three more labels.
Sort solid shapes again.

Try This!

Look around.
Find other solid shapes.
Sort them.

Activities

Shape Art

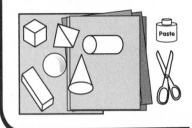

1. Choose a solid shape.
   Place it on the paper.
   Trace around a face
   of the shape.

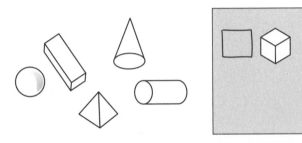

2. Trace more faces. Cut them out.

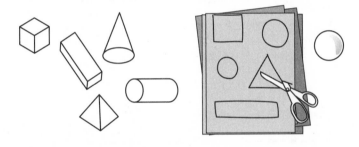

3. Make shape art.
   Put the faces on a sheet of paper.
   Paste them down.

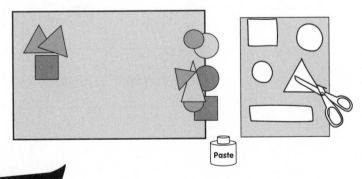

Try This!

Label each flat shape in your picture.
Give your picture a name.

Activities

Put It There

1. Pick a card. Read it.
   Use counters.
   Follow the direction.

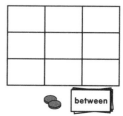

left

2. Find a matching word on your gameboard.
   Cover it.

right	left	over
right	over	under
between	under	left

left

3. Take turns.
   Cover three spaces
   in a row or column.

right	left	over
right	over	under
between	under	left

Try This!

Choose a card.
Draw a picture to show the position.

Slides, Flips, and Turns

What You'll Need:

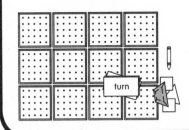

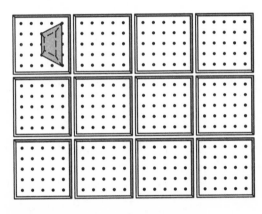

1. Choose a pattern block. Align it on the dots.

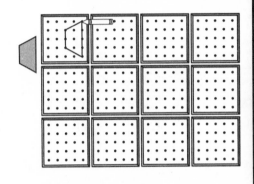

2. Trace the pattern block.

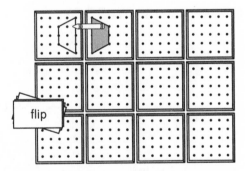

3. Your partner turns over a card. Do what the card says.

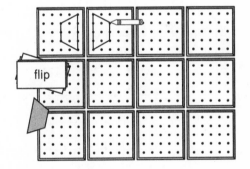

4. Trace the pattern block. Take turns.

Try This!

Draw a shape. Choose a card.
Your partner draws a slide, flip, or turn.

Patterns of the Past

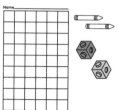
1. Look at the quilt.
Find the pattern.

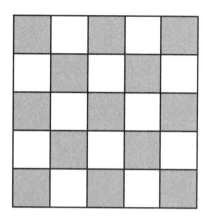

2. Use cubes.
Copy the pattern.

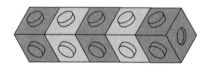

3. Color the pattern onto grid paper.
Use two colors.

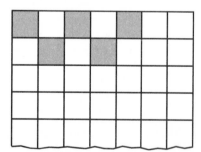

Try This!

**Copy the pattern with cubes.
What comes next?**

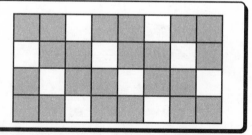

Picture Parts

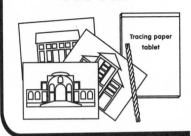

Tracing paper tablet

1. Look at the pictures. Use yarn. Make a line of symmetry.

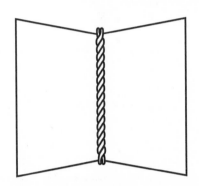

2. Fold tracing paper in half. Open it. Identify the line of symmetry.

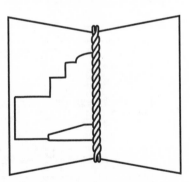

3. Draw half of a building. Fold the paper again. Turn it over.

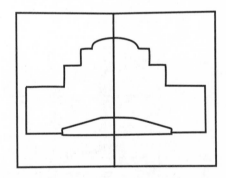

4. Your partner traces around your building. Open the paper.

Try This!

Show symmetry.
Add windows and doors
to each side.

Activities

Slice It Up

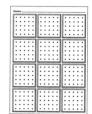
1. Draw a square.
Show two equal parts.

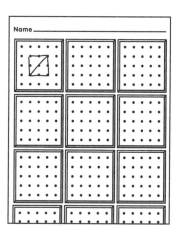

2. Draw another square.
Draw another way to
show two equal parts.

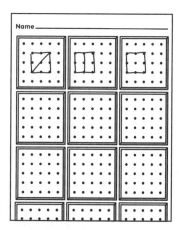

Can you show more
ways?

3. Draw more squares.
Show three equal
parts.

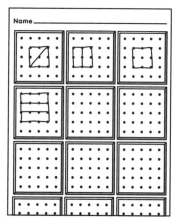

Try This!

Do the activity again.
Use a rectangle.
Show four equal parts.

It's a Puzzle

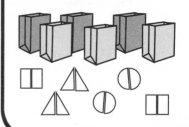

1. Pick a bag.
Take out parts.

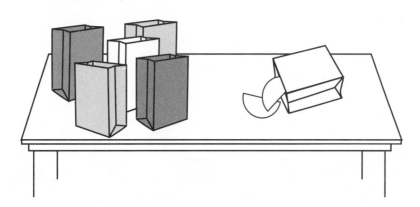

2. Put the parts together. Make a shape.
How many parts?

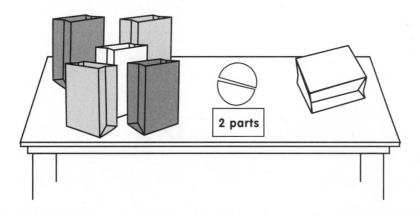

2 parts

3. Take turns with your partner. Keep playing.
Put the parts from each bag together.

Try This!

Put all the parts back into one bag.
Take out one part at a time.
Put together all six shapes.

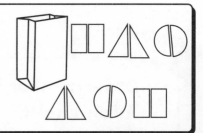

Follow Me

1. Color one part.
Don't let your partner see.

2. Your partner follows your directions. Tell what fraction to color. Tell what color.

3. Look at your partner's paper. Are equal parts colored? Talk about it.

4. Take turns being the leader.

Try This!

Draw another way to color the same fraction. Talk about it.

Cube Grab

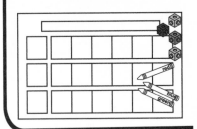

1. Look at the cubes.
   Which group has the most?

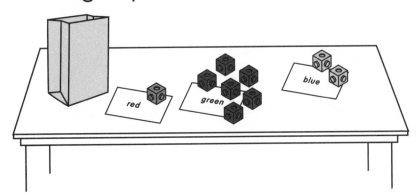

2. Place the cubes in the bag.
   Predict which cube you will pick.

3. Pick a
   cube out
   of the
   bag.
   What
   color is
   the cube?
   Color a
   box on
   the graph.
   Put the cube back in the bag.

4. Keep going until one row on the graph is full.

Try This!

**Use the same number of cubes for each color.
Repeat the activity. Does the graph look different?**

Activities

Spin and Count

What You'll Need:

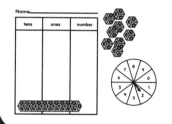

1. Build a 10 with red cubes.

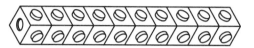

2. Spin. Count that many blue cubes.

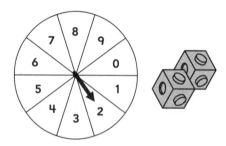

3. How many tens?
How many ones?
How many cubes in all?
Write the numbers.

tens	ones	number
1	2	12

Spin and play again.

Try This!

Draw a picture of 10 cubes.
Spin.
Draw that many ones.
Write the number.

Number Switch

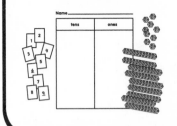
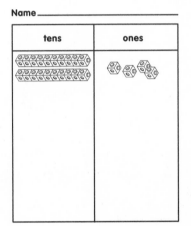

2 | **4**

1. Take two cards.
Make a number.

2. Show your number.
Use the blocks.

4 | **2**

3. Switch your cards.
Make a new number.

4. Show the number.
Use the blocks.

Pick two more cards.
Draw a picture of your number.

Roll and Write

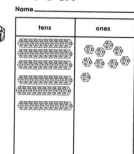

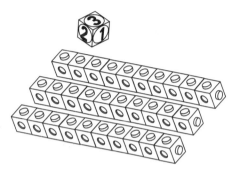

1. Roll the 1–6 cube. Your partner shows that many tens.

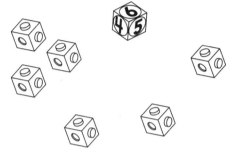

2. Roll the 4–9 cube. Your partner shows that many ones.

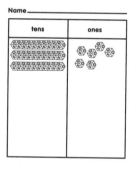

$$30 + 6 = 36$$

3. Tell how many tens and ones.

Roll the number cubes again. Show the numbers.

4. Show the number a different way.

Try This!

Switch the numbers in your last roll.
Write the tens and ones.
Write the number a different way.

Activities

Pick a Number

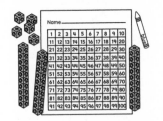

1. Pick some blocks.
Show a number.

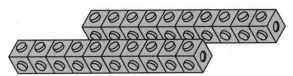

2. Color the number.

blue

3. Write how many.

I colored _____ numbers.

Try This!

Choose a number.
Draw the blocks that show the number.

Activities

Number Lineup

What You'll Need:

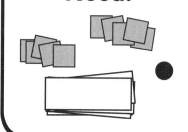

1. Line up 10 squares.

2. Place a counter on any square.
Count to find the position in line.

3. Find the ordinal number card.
Put it under the square.

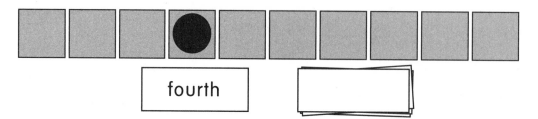

fourth

4. Try again. Take turns.

Try This!

**Put all the names
in order.
Start with first.**

first

second

Activities

Best Guess

1. Count a group of
10 paper clips.

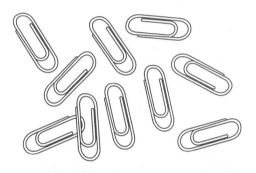

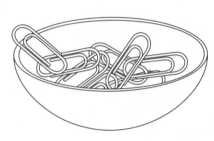

2. Make another group.
Use all the paper clips in the bowl.
Estimate how many in all.
Write your estimate.

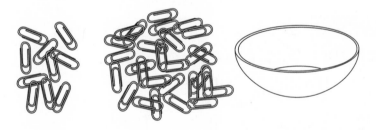

3. Count all the paper clips. Write the exact
number. Was your estimate close?

Try This!

Take a handful of paper clips.
Take 10 other paper clips.
Estimate which group has more.

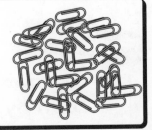

Missing Links

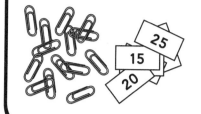

What You'll Need:

1. Make strings of
   5 paper clips.
   Count the strings
   by 5s.

2. Count again.
   Place a number card under each string.

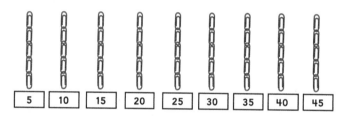

| 5 | 10 | 15 | 20 | 25 | 30 | 35 | 40 | 45 |

3. Take away one card.
   Your partner skip counts by 5s
   to find the missing number.

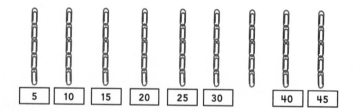

| 5 | 10 | 15 | 20 | 25 | 30 | | 40 | 45 |

4. Play again. Take turns.

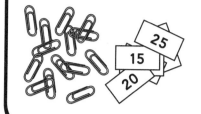

Try This!

Take away 2 cards.
Count by 5s to find the numbers.

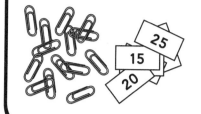

Activities

What's My Seat Number?

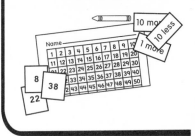

1. Choose a number card. Choose a word clue card.

2. Read the number and the clue to your partner.

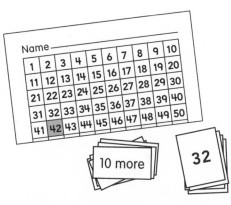

3. Your partner finds the seat number. Then your partner colors it on the chart.

4. Take turns. Play until you color 10 seat numbers.

Try This!

Think of a seat number. Say your seat is to the *left* or *right* of the number. Have your partner guess your seat number.

Odd or Even?

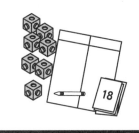

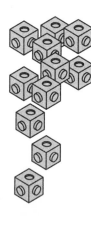

1. Pick a card. Count that many cubes.

2. Put the cubes in pairs.

odd	even
7	

3. Is the number odd or even? Write the number.

odd	even
7	4
3	20
15	

4. Take turns. Stop after 10 turns.

Try This!

You and a friend are sharing cookies.
Would 3 or 4 cookies be easier to share? Why?

Time for Fun

1. Think of an activity that is fun.

Activities

2. Show the start time on the first clock.

3. Show the end time on the second clock

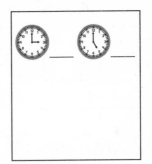

4. Write how long it takes. Draw a picture about the activity.

Try This!

Choose an activity that takes about 4 hours.
Draw a picture.

Dates and Days

What You'll Need:

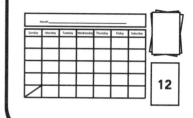

1. Pick a number card.

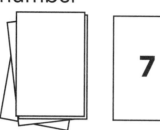

2. Find the number on the calendar.

Month	**May**					
Sunday	Monday	Tuesday	Wednesday	Thursday	Friday	Saturday
					1	2
3	4	5	6	7	8	9
10	11	12	13	14	15	16
17	18	19	20	21	22	23
24 / 31	25	26	27	28	29	30

7

3. Tell the day of the week. Take turns.

Month	**May**					
Sunday	Monday	Tuesday	Wednesday	Thursday	Friday	Saturday
					1	2
3	4	5	6	7	8	9
10	11	12	13	14	15	16
17	18	19	20	21	22	23
24 / 31	25	26	27	28	29	30

Thursday

Try This!

Play the game again. Tell the day of the week for each number. Then tell the day after.

Favorite Month

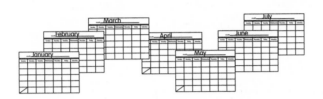

1. Look at a calendar.
Choose your favorite month.

2. Fill in the days of your favorite month.

Month **August**						
Sunday	Monday	Tuesday	Wednesday	Thursday	Friday	Saturday
						1
2	3	4	5	6	7	8
9	10	11	12	13	14	15
16	17	18	19	20	21	22
23	24	25	26	27	28	29
30	31					

3. Choose five days.
Draw pictures of some things you like to do.

Month **August**						
Sunday	Monday	Tuesday	Wednesday	Thursday	Friday	Saturday
						1
2	3	4	5	6	7	8
9	10	11	12	13	14	15
16	17	18	19	20	21	22
23	24	25	26	27	28	29
30	31					

4. Point to a picture on your partner's calendar.
Ask: "What day is this? What day is tomorrow?"

Try This!

Describe one day on your calendar.
Let your partner guess which day.

Activities

How Many Coins?

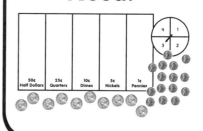

1. Put the pennies on the mat.
Put the nickels on the mat.

2. Spin the spinner.
Count that many pennies.
Take them off the mat.

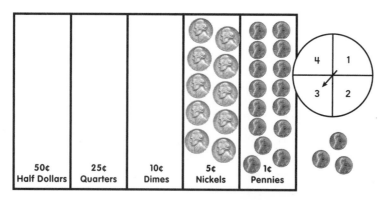

3. Take turns. When you get 5 pennies,
trade them for 1 nickel.

Keep playing.
Stop when each player gets 5 nickels.

Try This!

Count your money.
How much do you have?

Shopping Spree

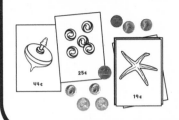

1. Look at the cards.

2. Choose a card. Read the amount.
Count coins to match.

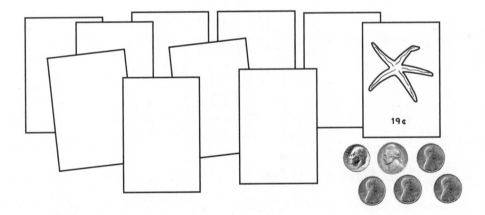

3. Check the amount.

Try This!

Play again.
Buy two items.
Which item has the greater value?

Shake in Step

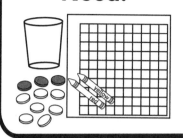

1. Shake and spill 10 counters.

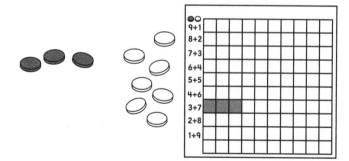

2. Put the reds in one group.
Put the yellows in another group.

	9+1
	8+2
	7+3
	6+4
	5+5
	4+6
	3+7
	2+8
	1+9

3. Match the counters to a problem.
Color the row red and yellow to match
the counters.

Try This!

Play again with 10 coins.
Count heads and tails.

Three in a Row

What You'll Need:

Activities

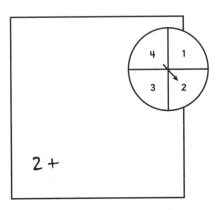

2 +

1. Spin.
Write the number
and +.

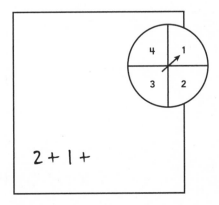

2 + 1 +

2. Spin again.
Write the number
and +.

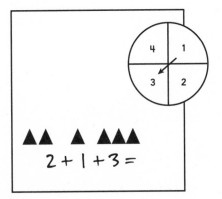

▲▲ ▲ ▲▲▲
2 + 1 + 3 =

3. Spin again.
Write the number
and =.

▲▲ ▲ ▲▲▲
2 + 1 + 3 = 6

4. Color shapes for
each number.
Write the sum.

Try This!

Show the sum 2 other ways.
Write the number sentences.

Pick a Part

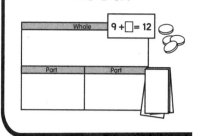

1. Pick a card.
Look at the sum.
Put that many counters
in the whole section.

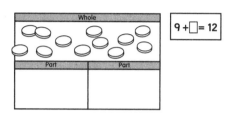

2. Now look at the first number. Move
that many counters to a part section.

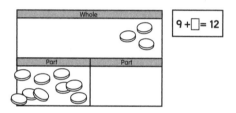

3. Move the rest of the counters to the
other part section. Count them.
What is the missing number?

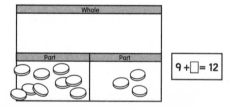

4. Pick another card.
Try again.

Try This!

Write another addition sentence for each card.
Use counters to check your sentence.

Hidden Numbers

1. Count out 11 counters.

2. Choose a card. Hide the counters.

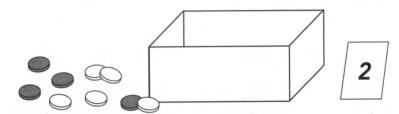

3. Count how many are left.
Ask your partner how many are hidden.

4. Check your partner's answer.

Try This!

Count and hide counters.
Write the subtraction fact.

Activities

Family in Counters

1. Put 11 counters in a cup.
Shake gently. Spill.

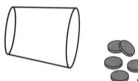

2. How many red? How many yellow?

3. Write the fact family.

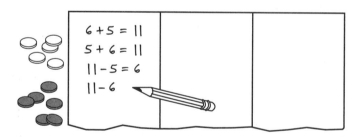

$$6 + 5 = 11$$
$$5 + 6 = 11$$
$$11 - 5 = 6$$
$$11 - 6$$

4. Shake and spill again.
Find more fact families.

Try This!

Place all your fact families face up.
Find fact families that are missing.
Make a fact family card.

What's in a Name?

1. Mix the cards.
Place them facedown.

2. Turn over two cards.
Do they name the same number?
Then keep both cards. Take another turn.

3. Do they name different numbers?
Then return the cards facedown.

4. Take turns.

Try This!

Choose two cards that name the same number.
Both partners take a new card.
Play with all the cards.

Activities

Guess and Measure

What You'll Need:

1. Take an object. Draw it.

2. Guess its length in cubes. Write your estimate.

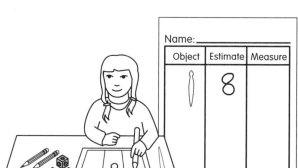

3. Measure with cubes. Write the measure. Were you close?

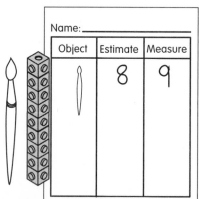

4. Try again. Estimate and measure. Are you getting closer?

Try This!

Find an object in the classroom that is 12 cubes long.

Activities

List the Lengths

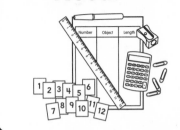

1. Pick a number card.

Look around the room.
Guess which object is that many inches long.

2. Measure. Write on the chart.

Name: _____		
Number	Object	Length
5	marker	

3. Try again. Pick new cards.

Try This!

Measure your thumb with a ruler.
Use your thumb to measure objects.

Activities

Weighing In

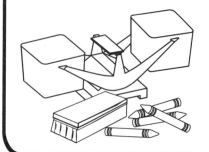

1. Put an eraser on one side.

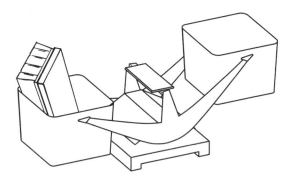

2. Put crayons on the other side.

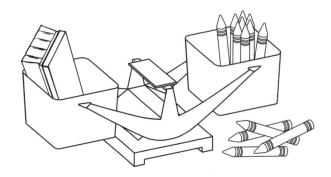

3. Add or take out crayons. Make both sides balance.

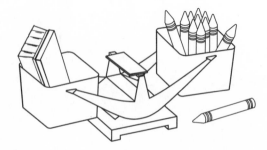

Try This!

Try to balance crayons and cubes.

Activities

More or Less

1. Fill a container with rice.

2. Take another container.
Will it hold more or less? Guess.

3. Pour in the rice. Were you correct?

Try again. Use other containers.
Guess and check.

Try This!

Choose 3 containers.
Put them in order from least to greatest amount.
Check to find out if the order is correct.

Activities

Dress for Success

1. Look at the card.
What is the temperature?

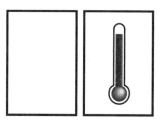

2. Draw an outdoor picture. Put people in the picture. Dress them for the temperature.

Try This!

Look at the other card.
Tell a story about what you might do when it is this temperature.

Activities

Frame 10

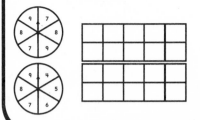
1. Spin the 7–9 spinner. Put that many red cubes on the mat.

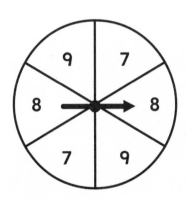

2. Spin the 4–9 spinner. Put that many green cubes on the mat.

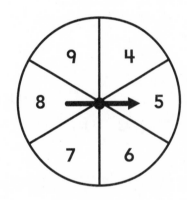

3. How many cubes are there in all?

Try This!

Draw a picture to show one of your spins.

Activities

Number Groups

What You'll Need:

1. Write a number from 11 to 18. Show that many cubes.

14

2. Put the cubes into two groups. Write the number sentence.

| 14 |
| 6 + 8 = 14 |

3. Use the same number. Change the groups. Make more number sentences.

| 14 |
| 6 + 8 = 14 |
| 9 + 5 = 14 |

4. Now write another number. Write more number sentences.

 **Try This!**

Write a number. Put the cubes into 3 groups.
Show and write other number sentences.

Activities

Double Spin

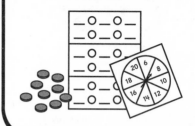

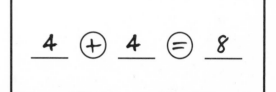

1. Spin the spinner. Show the counters in pairs.

2. Write the addition sentence.

$4 \oplus 4 \ominus 8$

3. Take away one row. How many are left?

4. Write a subtraction sentence.

$4 \oplus 4 \ominus 8$

$8 \ominus 4 \ominus 4$

5. Take turns. Repeat the activity.

Try This!

Draw an even number of animals.
Draw them in two rows.
Circle one row.
Write the subtraction sentence.

Subtraction Cubes

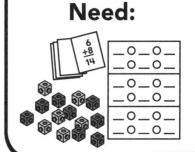

1. Place cards in a pile facedown. Choose a card.

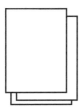

$$\begin{array}{r} 6 \\ +8 \\ \hline 14 \end{array}$$

2. Show the addition fact with cubes.

$$\begin{array}{r} 6 \\ +8 \\ \hline 14 \end{array}$$

3. Write the addition fact. Write a related addition fact.

$6 \oplus 8 = 14$

$8 \oplus 6 = 14$

$14 \ominus 6 = 8$

$14 \ominus 8 = 6$

$\_\_ \bigcirc \_\_ = \_\_$

$\_\_ \bigcirc \_\_ = \_\_$

4. Write the related subtraction facts.

Try This!

Write your own fact card. Have your partner write all the related facts.

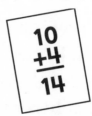

$$\begin{array}{r} 10 \\ +4 \\ \hline 14 \end{array}$$

Missing Numbers

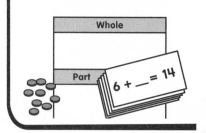

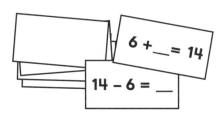

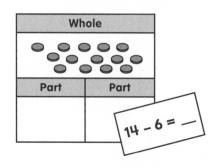

Activities

1. Turn over a pair of cards. Look at the subtraction.

2. What is the whole? Put that many counters on the mat.

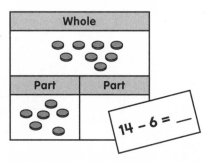

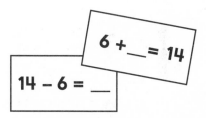

3. What part do you take away? Move that many counters to the part section.

4. Use the subtraction fact to find the missing addend.

5. Switch roles. Play again.

Write related fact cards.
Have your partner find the missing numbers.

Tens and Tens

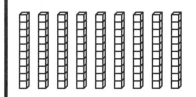

1. Pick some tens.
Your partner picks some.

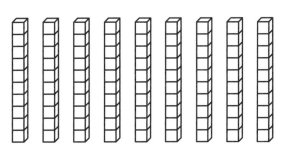

2. How many tens did
you pick?
What is your
number?
Tell your partner.

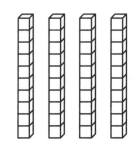

3. Add your tens to
your partner's tens.
How many tens are
there in all?
What is the sum?

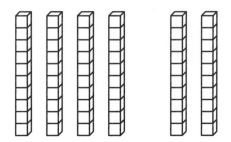

4. Take turns going first.

Try This!

Play again.
Use connecting cubes to build 9 trains.
Make each train 10 cubes long.

Roll into Place

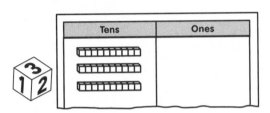
1. Roll the number cube. Your partner shows how many tens.

2. Spin the spinner. Your partner shows how many ones.

3. Spin the spinner again. Your partner adds that many ones.

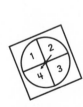

4. Add. Tell the sum.

5. Take turns. Roll the number cubes again. Show the numbers on the mat.

Draw a picture to show your work.

Activities

Pick and Spin

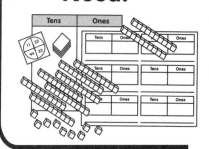

1. Pick a card. Show how many tens. Show how many ones.

Tens	Ones

24

2. Spin the spinner. Show how many tens. Show how many ones.

Tens	Ones

3. Add. Write the sum.

Tens	Ones

Tens	Ones		Tens	Ones
4	6			

Tens	Ones		Tens	Ones

Tens	Ones		Tens	Ones

4. Try again. Pick another card. Spin another number.

Try This!

Write a story for your exercise.

Rolling Away

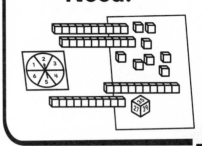

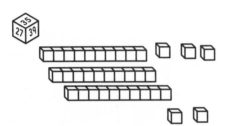

1. Roll the cube. Show the number with place-value blocks.

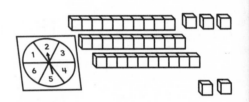

2. Spin the spinner. Take away that many blocks.

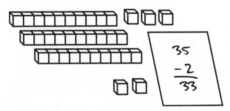

3. What is the difference? Have your partner write the subtraction.

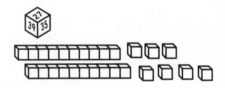

4. Switch roles. Keep playing. Write the subtraction each time.

Try This!

Try subtracting first.
Then use blocks to check.

Number Boxes

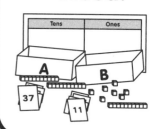

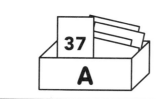

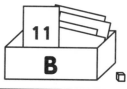

1. Pick a card from Box A. Use blocks to show that number.

2. Pick a card from Box B. Take away the ones first.

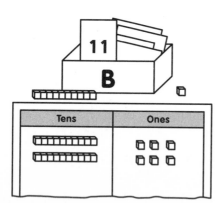

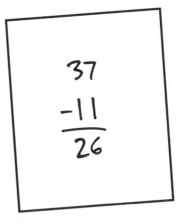

$$\begin{array}{r} 37 \\ -11 \\ \hline 26 \end{array}$$

3. Take away the tens.

4. Write the subtraction. Try again. Use other cards.

Try This!

Show any number on the mat.
Take away 1 ten.
Write the subtraction.

Spin Away

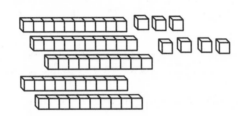

1. Spin the spinner.
Use blocks.
Show the number.

2. Spin the other spinner.
Take away that many blocks.

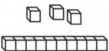

3. What is the difference?
Write the subtraction
problem.

$$57 \\ -13 \\ \overline{44}$$

4. Keep trying.
Write 4 subtraction problems.

Try This!

Play again.
Try adding first.
Use blocks to check.

Name _____

Spotlight on: 3

1. Count.
Write the
number.

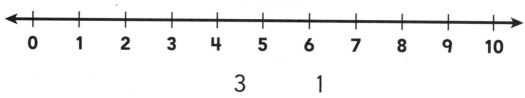

__1__   _____   _____   _____ butterflies

---

2. Circle the number that is less.

```
←——+——+——+——+——+——+——+——+——+——+——+——→
   0   1   2   3   4   5   6   7   8   9   10
```

        3   1

---

3. Write the numbers.

just before   between   just after

____, 4, 5   12, ____, 14   2, 3, ____

---

4. Talk About It Circle the words
that make the sentence correct.
   Shayna has 5 buttons.
   Ellie has 3 buttons.

Shayna   **Ellie**

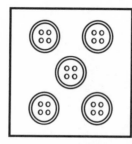   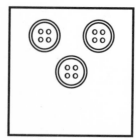

is greater than

5   3

is less than

Number of the Week

Name _____

Spotlight on:

1. Add.
Write the number.

2   **3**

$2 + 3 =$ _____ bananas

---

2. Karim eats 4 pancakes.
Then he eats 1 more.
How many pancakes does
Karim eat?

_____ + _____ = _____

_____ pancakes

---

3. Find the shape
with five sides.
Draw a line
under it.

---

4. Talk About It Use cubes to find how long.

Jenny's crayon is 3 cubes long.
José's crayon is 2 cubes longer.
How long is José's crayon?
Tell how you found out.

Name _____

Spotlight on:  7

1. Circle and cross out to subtract.
Write the difference.

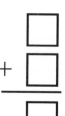

$$7 - 6 = \underline{\quad}$$

---

2. Write the addition fact two ways.

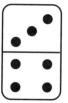

$$\underline{\quad} + \underline{\quad} = \underline{\quad}$$

---

3. Which box has seven crayons?
Circle it.

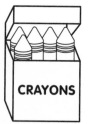   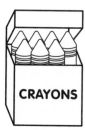   CRAYONS   CRAYONS   CRAYONS

---

4. Talk About It

7 eggs are in a nest.
2 eggs hatch into chicks.
How many eggs are left?
Tell how you know.

Name _____

Spotlight on: (8)

1. Draw 8 circles. Draw 3 squares.
Write how many shapes in all.

_____ shapes

2. Belle has 6 baseball cards.
Shira has 8 cards.
Who has more cards?

_____

3. Use the bar graph.

How many children like
orange juice?

_____ children

How many like grape juice?

_____ children

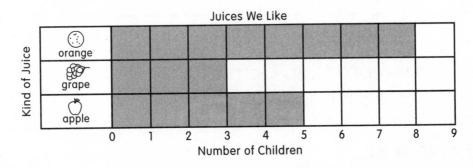

4. Talk About It How many more children
like orange juice than apple juice?

Number of the Week

Spotlight on: 6

1. Look at the pictograph.

Lost Teeth

3 teeth	☺ ☺ ☺ ☺ ☺ ☺
2 teeth	☺ ☺ ☺ ☺
1 tooth	☺ ☺ ☺ ☺ ☺

Each ☺ stands for 1 child.

How many children have lost three teeth? _____ children

2. Count and tally.

Raindrops

How many raindrops? _____ raindrops

3. Gemma lost 2 teeth.
Noel lost 4 more than Gemma.
How many teeth has Noel lost? _____ teeth

4. Talk About It

Chris has 1 stamp.
Sara has 6 stamps.
What number will you start with to add the two numbers?
Why is it helpful to start with that number?

Name _____

Spotlight on: 9

1. Circle the numbers that are greater than 9.

5   12   6   18   10

_____

2. Count backwards.
Fill in the missing numbers.

9, _____, _____, _____, 5, 4, 3, 2, 1

_____

3. Circle the one that shows nine tally marks.

_____

4. Talk About It How many triangles
can you make with 9 sticks?

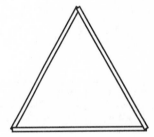

Spotlight on: 4

1. Draw a shape with 4 corners.

_____

2. Cary has 4 circles.
Ina has 4 more circles than Cary.
Show how many circles Ina
has in all.

Draw a picture.

3. How many more cubes does Cara
have than Dillon?

_____ cubes

Number of Cubes

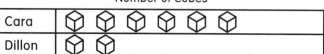

| Cara | 🔲 🔲 🔲 🔲 🔲 🔲 |
| Dillon | 🔲 🔲 |

4. Talk About It

Look at the square.
Make 4 triangles in the square.
Use 2 lines only.

Name _____

Spotlight on: ②

1. Draw 2 hearts over the star.
Draw 2 circles to the left
of the star.

---

2. Look at the tally chart.
How many more baskets
did Ella get than Adam?

Basketball Tally	
Ella	Adam
卌 卌	卌 卌
卌 ‖	卌

_____ baskets

---

3. Jane has 7 bows.
She gives away 5 bows.
How many bows are left?

_____ bows

---

4. **Talk About It** Mai sews
this pattern on a quilt.
Draw the next pattern unit.

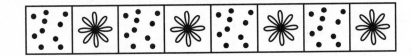

Name _____

Spotlight on: $\frac{1}{2}$

1. Color to show $\frac{1}{2}$.

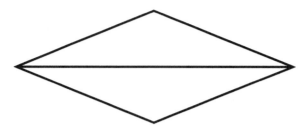

---

2. Nicki has 4 marbles.
$\frac{1}{2}$ of the marbles are red.
Color to show how many
marbles are red.

---

3. Draw a square.
Color to show $\frac{1}{2}$.

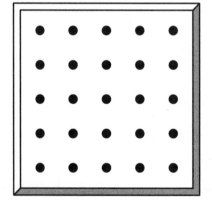

---

4. Write About It How can
you show $\frac{1}{2}$ of a set?

Number of the Week

Name _____

Spotlight on: (10)

1. Complete the fact family.

Whole	
10	
Part	**Part**
8	2

____ + ____ = ____   ____ − ____ = ____

____ + ____ = ____   ____ − ____ = ____

2. Use the bar graph to solve.

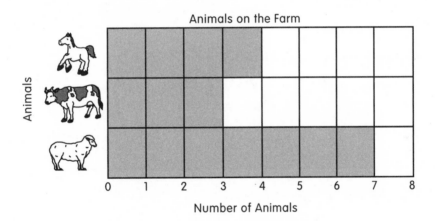

Animals on the Farm

How many sheep and cows are there? ____

3. Color to show $\frac{1}{2}$.

4. Talk About It Draw a line of symmetry. Tell how you know.

10

Spotlight on: 99

1. Write >, <, or =.

99 ◯ 96

---

2. Write the number that comes just after 99.

99, ____

---

3. Estimate. Circle the answer that makes sense.

Gina holds all her marbles in one hand. About how many marbles does Gina have?

about 9 marbles   about 99 marbles

---

4. Talk About It Count the tally marks. Circle a group of ten. Estimate how many in all. Then count.

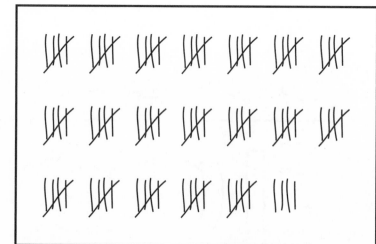

Estimate
____
Count
____

Number of the Week

Name _____

Spotlight on:  (50)

1. Skip count by 5s.
Write how many petals in all.

✸ ✸ ✸ ✸ ✸ ✸ ✸ ✸ ✸ ✸

_____ petals

---

2. The class collects 40 stamps.
Ty brings 10 more stamps.
Draw the tally marks on the chart.

Stamps We Collected

Count how many stamps in all?   _____ stamps

---

3. Circle the number that comes next.

50   40   30   50   40   30   50   40   _____

30

50

---

4. Talk About It Look at the spinner.
Are you more likely or less likely
to spin 50?
Tell why.

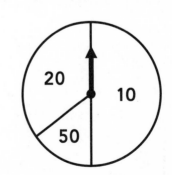

Number of the Week

Name_____

Spotlight on: 30

1. List three things that take about 30 minutes to do.

_____

_____

_____

2. Look at a calendar for a whole year.
Write the months that have only 30 days.

_____ _____

_____ _____

3. Count by 2s. Write the missing numbers.

22, 24, _____, _____, 30, _____

4. Talk About It Which is longer?
30 paper clips placed end to end
30 new pencils placed end to end

Number of the Week

Name _____

Spotlight on: 25

1. Write the missing numbers.

5, 10, _____, 20, _____, 30, 35

---

2. Greta and Bill save coins.
Who has the coins with
the greatest value?

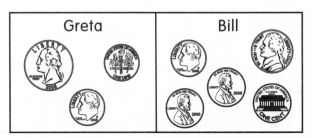

_____

---

3. Amy is having a party tomorrow.
Today is Tuesday, May 24.
On what day is Amy
having a party?

_____

Month		May				
Sunday	Monday	Tuesday	Wednesday	Thursday	Friday	Saturday
1	2	3	4	5	6	7
8	9	10	11	12	13	14
15	16	17	18	19	20	21
22	23	24	25	26	27	28
29	30					

Number of the Week

---

4. Talk About It

Carlos has 35¢.
He spends two coins.
He has these coins left.

What coins did he spend?

_____

Name _____

Spotlight on: (12)

1. Kim and his friends have 12¢.
Elaine has 1 nickel. Sue has 1 nickel.
What coins does Kim have?
Draw the coins to solve.

Kim has _____.

2. Look at the pictograph.

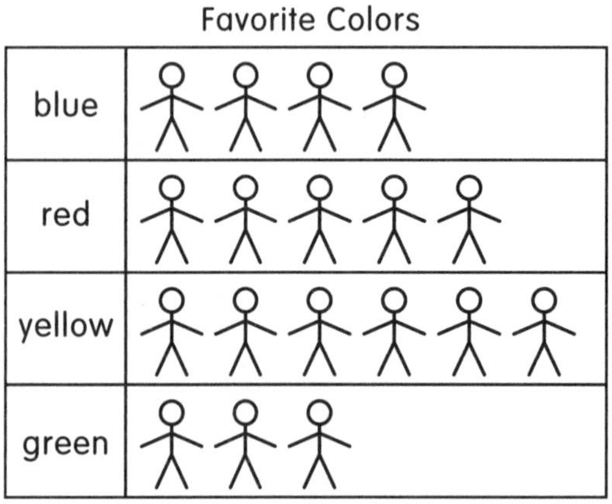

Each  👤 stands for one child.
How many children chose blue, green, and red?

Favorite Colors

blue	👤 👤 👤 👤
red	👤 👤 👤 👤 👤
yellow	👤 👤 👤 👤 👤 👤
green	👤 👤 👤

_____ children

3. Find the missing number.
$5 + \underline{} = 12$

4. Write About It Jack has 6 eggs.
How many more eggs does he need to make 12 eggs?
Write to show how you found the answer.

_____

_____

Number of the Week

Name _____

Spotlight on: (11)

1. Raina was sorting pattern blocks.
Look at her graph. How many more
circles than squares does she have?

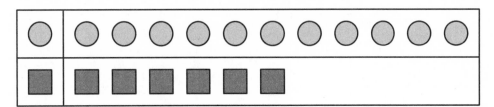

_____ circles

---

2. Kari has a piano lesson at 10:00.
It lasts for one hour.
What time does her lesson end?

_____

Number of the Week

---

3. Complete the fact family.

2 + _____ = 11   11 − _____ = 2

9 + _____ = 11   11 − _____ = 9

---

4. Talk About It

Janice and Jon want
to share the counters.
Can they each have
the same amount? Why?

Name _____

Spotlight on: 24

1. Write the missing numbers.

26, _____, 22, _____, 18, 16

2. Look at the tally chart. Who has 24 toy airplanes?

_____

Toy Planes

Ricardo	𝍤 𝍤 𝍤 I			
Linda	𝍤 𝍤 𝍤 𝍤 IIII			
Ken	𝍤 𝍤 𝍤 𝍤			

3. What number are you more likely to spin?

_____

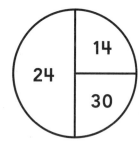

14
24
30

4. Talk About It

Is this page taller or shorter than 24 centimeters?

_____

Explain how you know.

Number of the Week

Spotlight on: 37

1. Circle groups of 10 marbles.

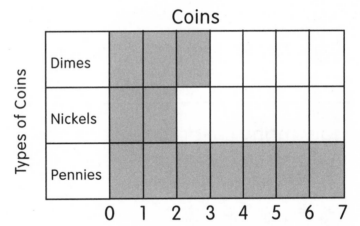

How many tens? _____

How many ones? _____

How many marbles in all? _____

2. Find the value of the coins.

_____ ¢

Coins

Types of Coins	0	1	2	3	4	5	6	7
Dimes								
Nickels								
Pennies								

3. Circle the number that is less.

37   **40**

4. Talk About It A child in Mr. Tom's class says there are 37 days in August.

Is the child correct? _____
How do you know?

Number of the Week

Name _____

Spotlight on: **18**

1. A stick is 18 inches long.
A pole is 21 inches long.
Circle the one that is longer.

stick   pole

_____

2. Find the sum.

```
   6
   8
+  4
_____
```

_____

Number of the Week

3. How many children walk to school?

How We Get to School	
🚲	ⅢⅢⅢ ⅢⅢⅢ ⅢⅢⅢ
🚶	ⅢⅢⅢ ⅢⅢⅢ ⅢⅢⅢ |||
🚌	ⅢⅢⅢ |||

_____ children

_____

4. Talk About It Are there more cubes or spheres?
Tell how you know.

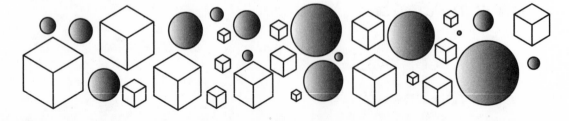

Name _____

Spotlight on: 15

1. Find how many groups of 3.

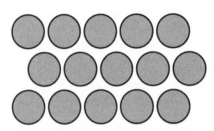

_____ groups of 3

2. Look at the cubes. Write a fact family.

3. Find who read more books.

_____

Write how many more.

Books Read

Carlos

Beth

0 1 2 3 4 5 6 7 8 9 10 11 12 13 14 15 16

Number of Books

_____

4. Talk About It Write the missing numbers. How did you find the missing numbers?

_____, _____, 15, 20, 25, _____, _____,

Spotlight on: 49

1. Write the numbers that come just before and just after.

   _____, 49, _____

2. 49 was moved in the following way. Was the move a slide, a flip, or a turn?

   49 49

   _____

Number of the Week

3. Circle the object that weighs about 1 pound.

Green Beans

4. **Write About It** Could you use mental math to add 40 + 9? Why?

   _____

   _____

   _____

Name_____

Spotlight on: 36

1. Circle the even number.

36   63

---

2. Find the missing number.

30 + □ = 36

---

3. 36 children are at the zoo.
Use tally marks to show
the number of children
who are at the zoo.

---

4. Talk About It Circle hot or cold to tell about the
temperature.

36 degrees

hot   cold

Tell how you know.

2-Column Chart

Resources

3-Column Chart

Resources

10 × 10 Grid Paper

4 +8	8 +4	4 +3	9 +2	7 +0
6 +3	2 +9	7 +4	3 +5	8 +3
3 +9	9 +3	7 +5	6 +5	5 +6
6 +4	9 +1	1 +8	3 +8	6 +6
7 +2	4 +7	4 +6	5 +7	8 +2

Resources

Addition Facts Through 12

8 +8	10 +10	7 +8	7 +5	5 +8
7 +7	7 +9	10 +7	4 +8	9 +8
10 +9	6 +9	8 +6	9 +7	7 +6
10 +5	5 +9	10 +3	10 +8	8 +5
9 +4	9 +9	8 +9	9 +6	9 +5

Addition Facts Through 20

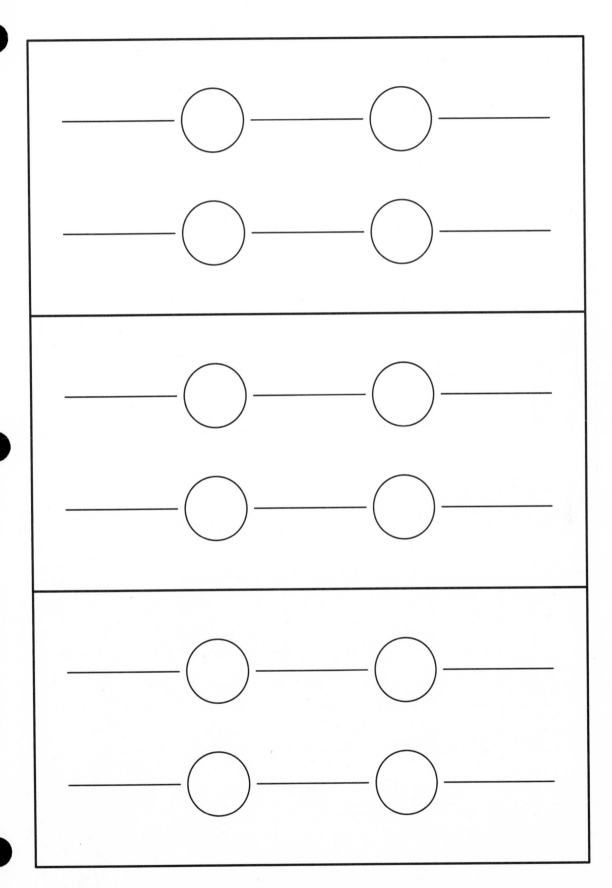

Addition/Subtraction Sentences

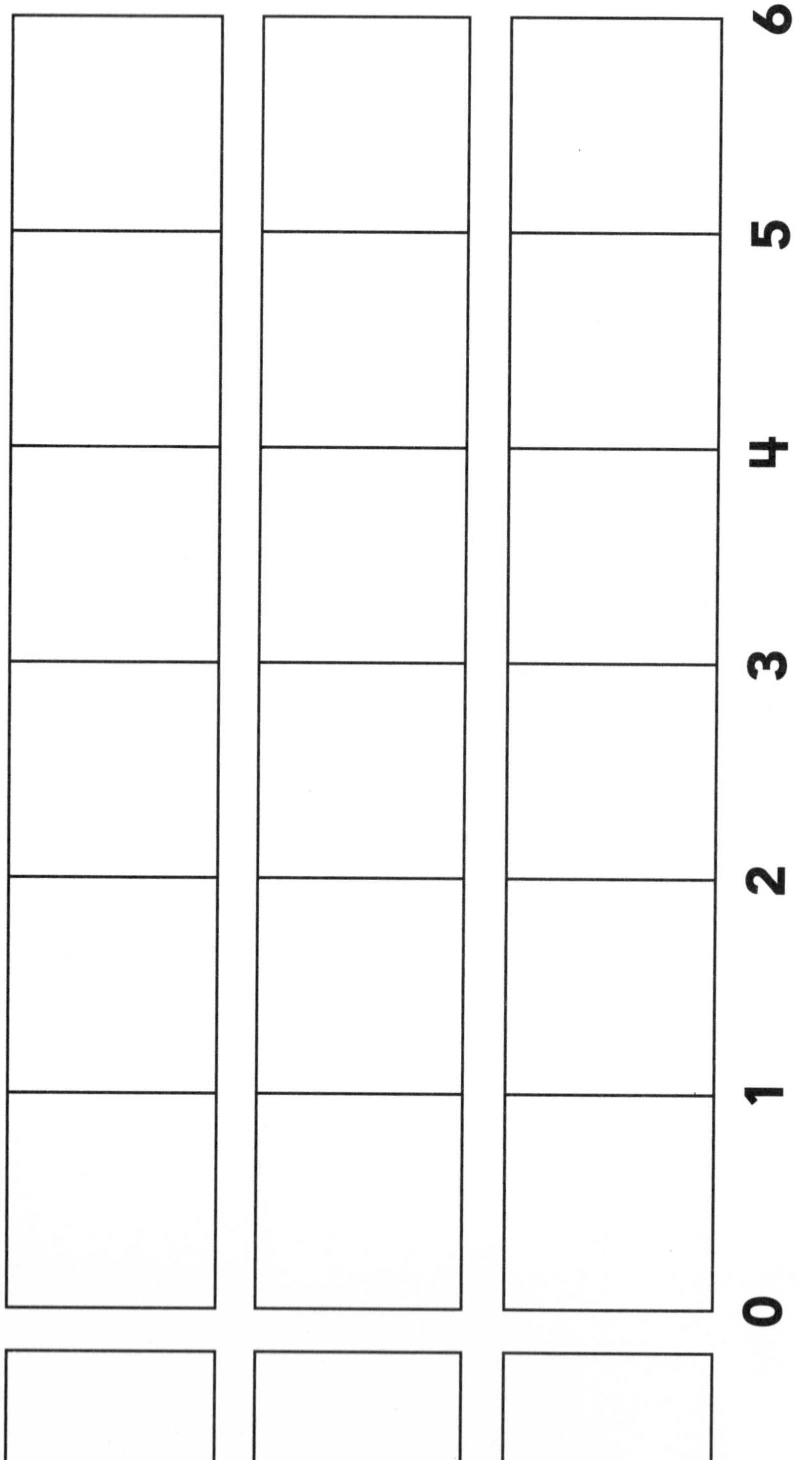

0 1 2 3 4 5 6

Bar Graph [3-Row]

0   1   2   3   4   5   6   7   8

month _____

Sunday	Monday	Tuesday	Wednesday	Thursday	Friday	Saturday

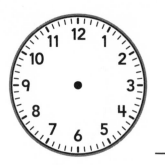

_____

_____

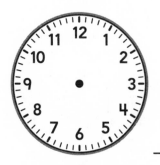

_____

_____

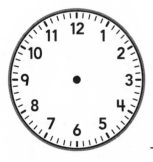

_____

_____

Clock Faces

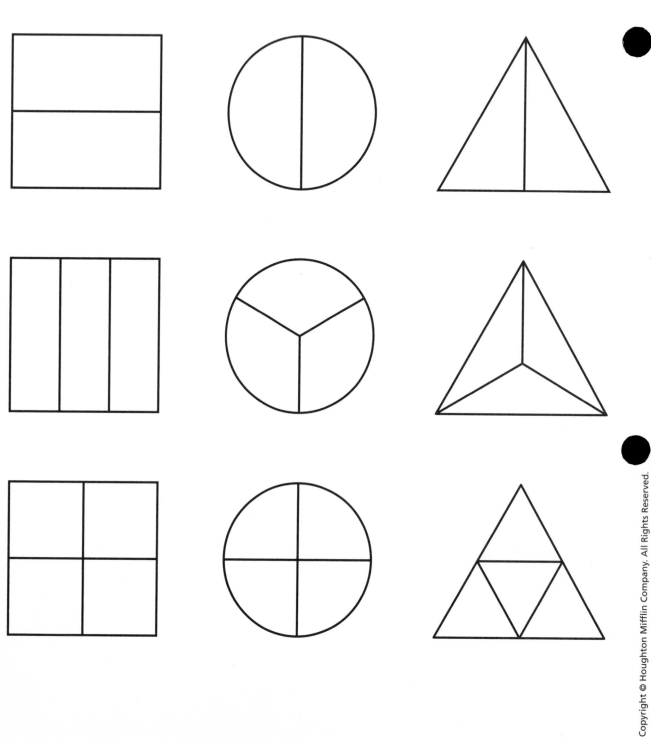

Resources

Fractions $\frac{1}{2}$, $\frac{1}{3}$, $\frac{1}{4}$

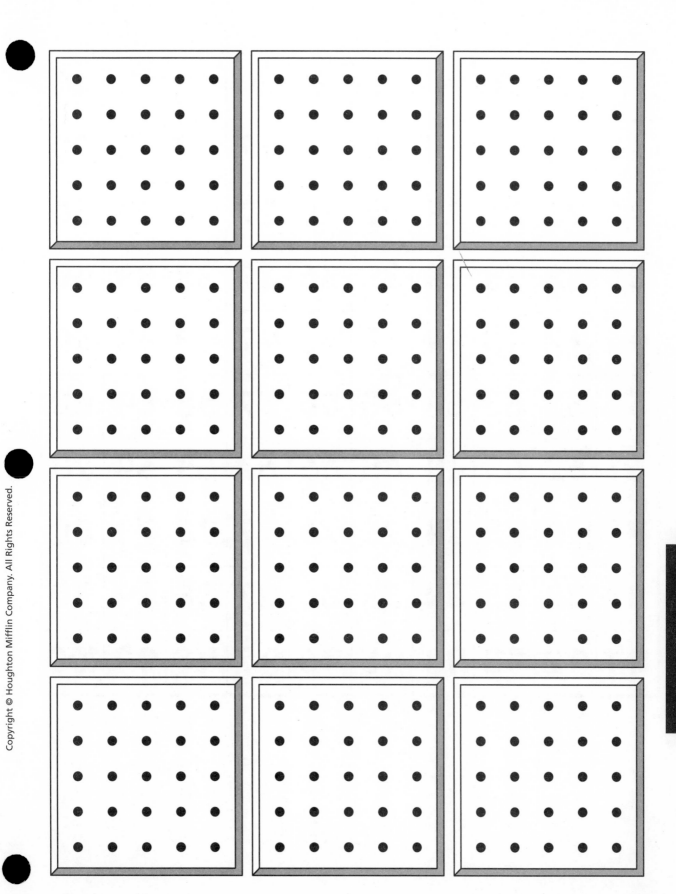

Geoboard Dot Paper

1	2	3	4	5	6	7	8	9	10
11	12	13	14	15	16	17	18	19	20
21	22	23	24	25	26	27	28	29	30
31	32	33	34	35	36	37	38	39	40
41	42	43	44	45	46	47	48	49	50
51	52	53	54	55	56	57	58	59	60
61	62	63	64	65	66	67	68	69	70
71	72	73	74	75	76	77	78	79	80
81	82	83	84	85	86	87	88	89	90
91	92	93	94	95	96	97	98	99	100

Hundred Chart

Resources

Inch Grid Paper

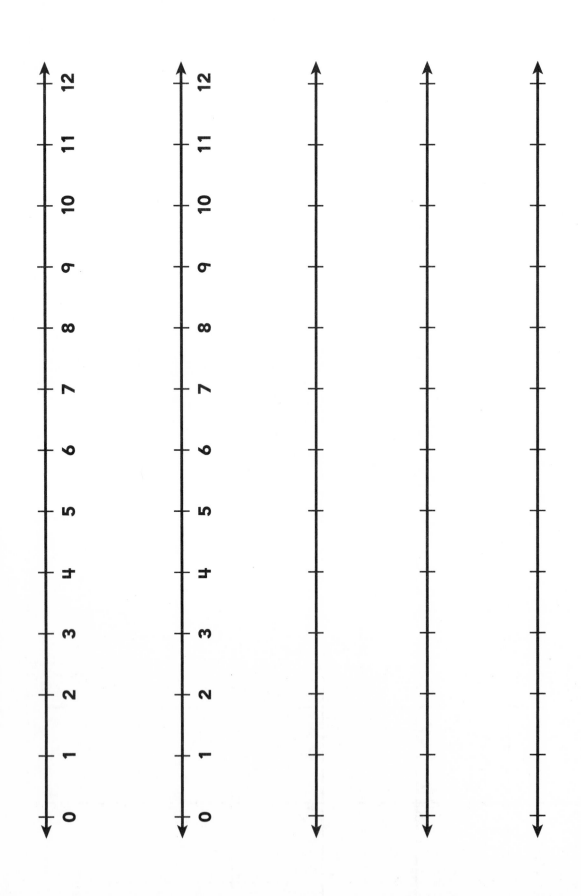

Number Lines

Whole	
Part	Part

Whole	
Part	Part

Whole	
Part	Part

Whole	
Part	Part

Pictograph

Tens	Ones

Tens	Ones

_____

_____

Tens	Ones

Tens	Ones

_____

_____

Tens	Ones

Tens	Ones

_____

_____

Resources

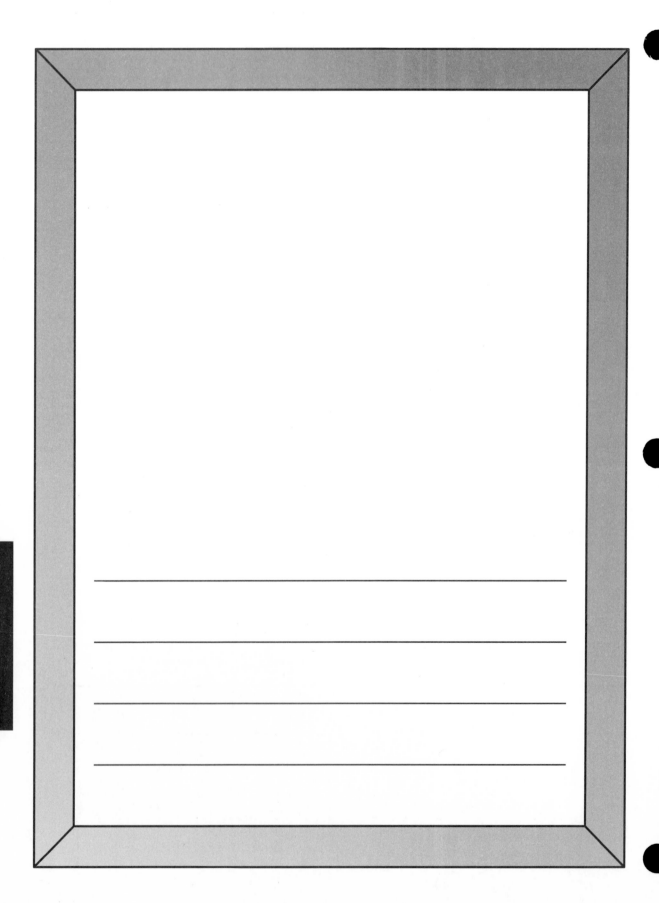

Resources

Story Mat

9 −0	10 −9	7 −6	8 −4	8 −6	4 −3
7 −1	5 −3	5 −1	3 −2	5 −4	8 −1
4 −2	8 −5	10 −1	2 −1	5 −2	7 −5
8 −7	6 −5	6 −4	8 −3	10 −2	6 −2
6 −1	7 −3	9 −1	9 −2	3 −1	8 −8
10 −8	8 −2	6 −3	7 −2	7 −4	9 −8

Resources

9 −5	10 −3	11 −2	12 −5	9 −3
12 −7	11 −8	11 −9	11 −4	10 −5
11 −5	10 −4	11 −3	9 −6	10 −7
12 −3	11 −7	10 −6	12 −8	9 −7
9 −4	11 −6	12 −4	12 −6	12 −9

Resources

Subtraction Facts Through 12

16 −9	13 −4	15 −7	15 −9	18 −9	14 −7
13 −6	18 −10	19 −10	14 −8	16 −7	11 −3
16 −6	11 −5	14 −6	12 −6	15 −8	14 −9
13 −5	13 −8	12 −4	17 −10	14 −4	13 −9
20 −10	17 −9	19 −9	15 −10	13 −7	12 −7
15 −5	16 −8	17 −8	18 −8	14 −5	15 −6

Subtraction Facts Through 20

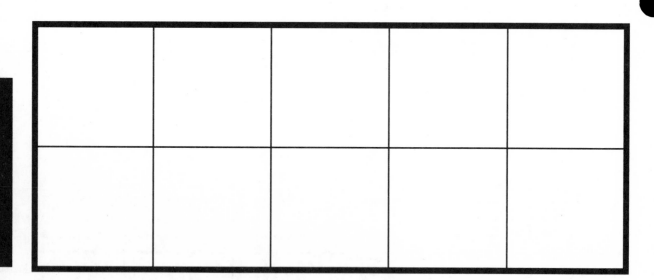

Ten Frame Sheet

Analog Clock Cards

Resources

Analog Clock Cards

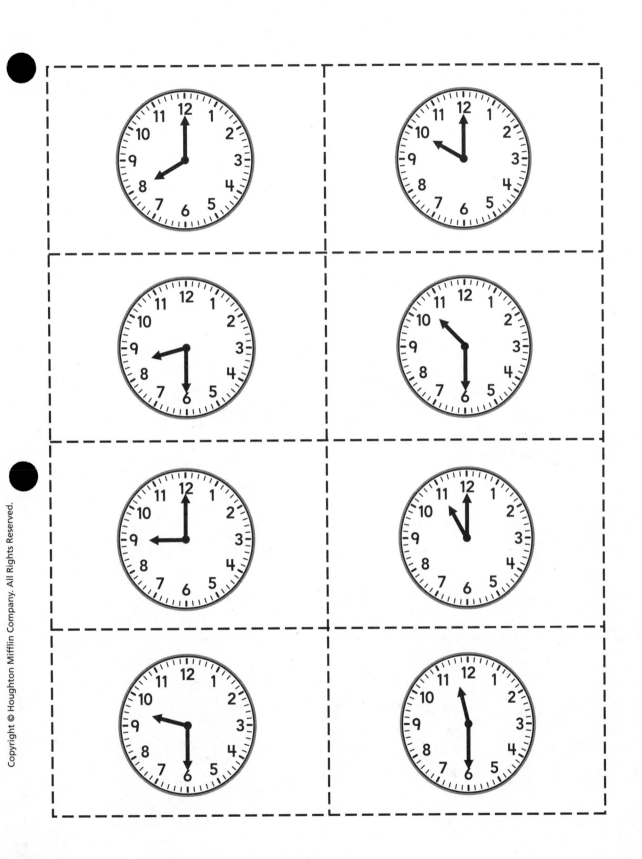

Analog Clock Cards

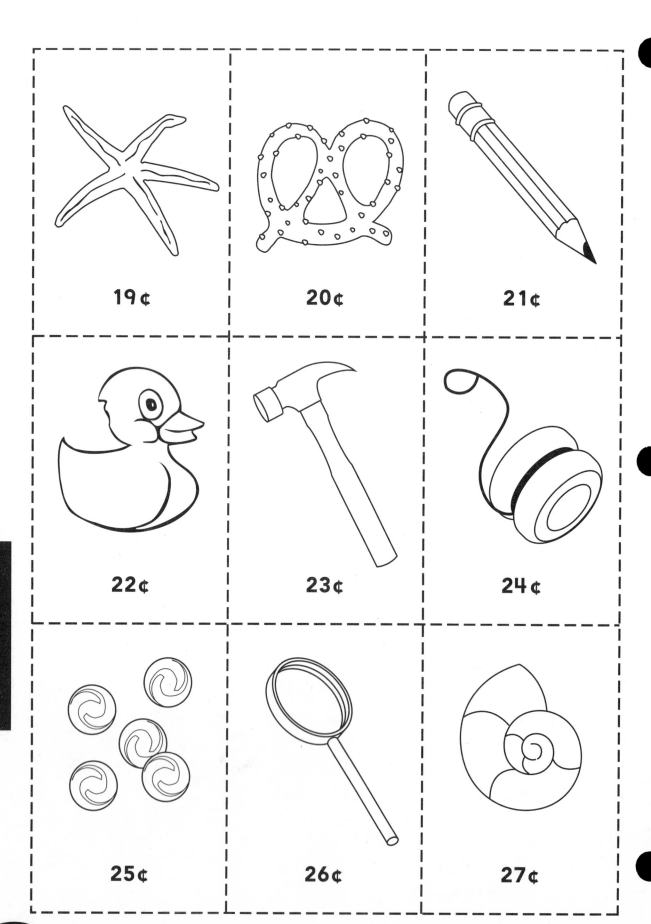

19¢

20¢

21¢

22¢

23¢

24¢

25¢

26¢

27¢

Resources

Class Store Cards

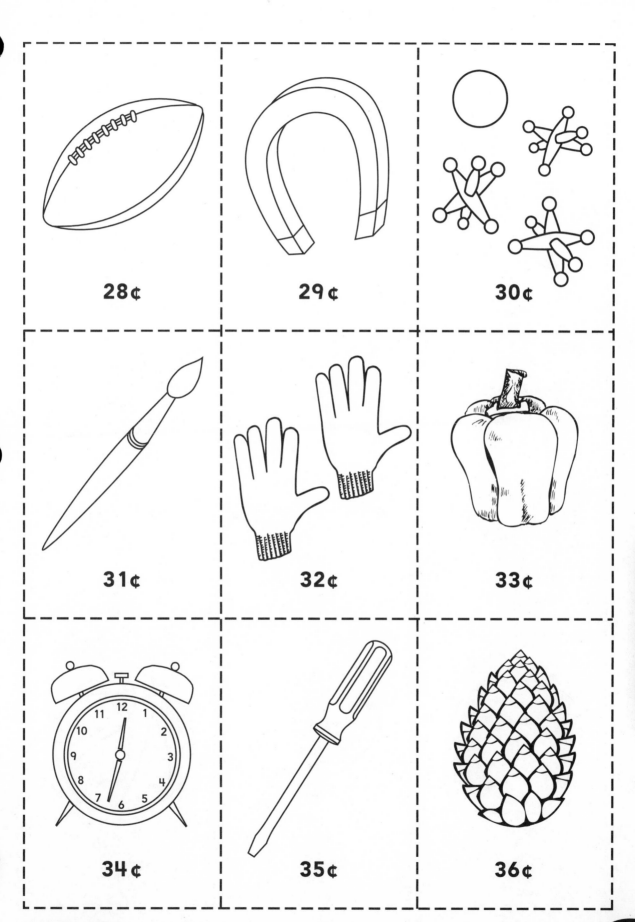

28¢

29¢

30¢

31¢

32¢

33¢

34¢

35¢

36¢

Resources

Class Store Cards

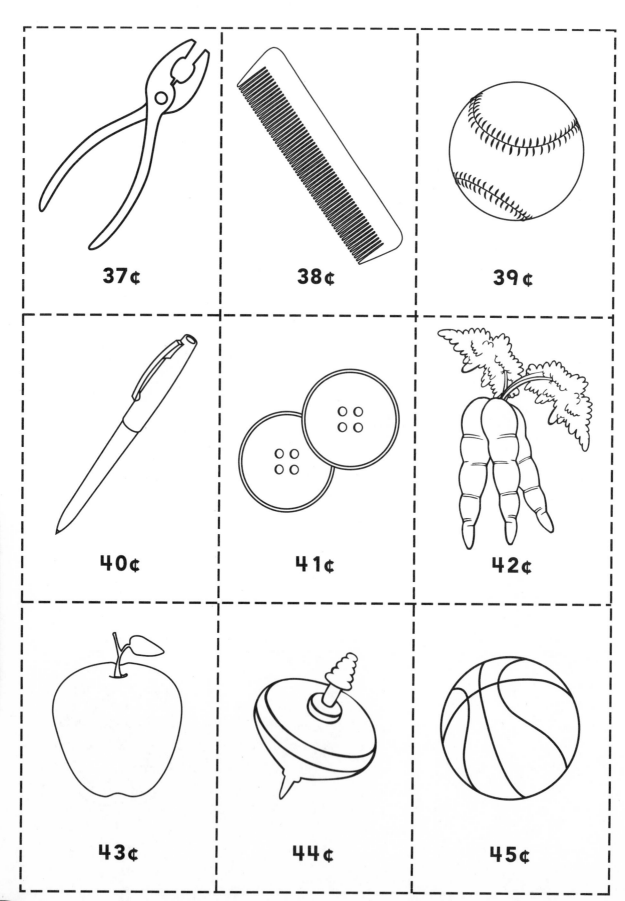

37¢

38¢

39¢

40¢

41¢

42¢

43¢

44¢

45¢

Class Store Cards

12:00

2:00

12:30

2:30

1:00

3:00

1:30

3:30

Resources

Digital Clock Cards

4:00	6:00
4:30	6:30
5:00	7:00
5:30	7:30

Digital Clock Cards

8:00	10:00
8:30	10:30
9:00	11:00
9:30	11:30

Resources

Digital Clock Cards

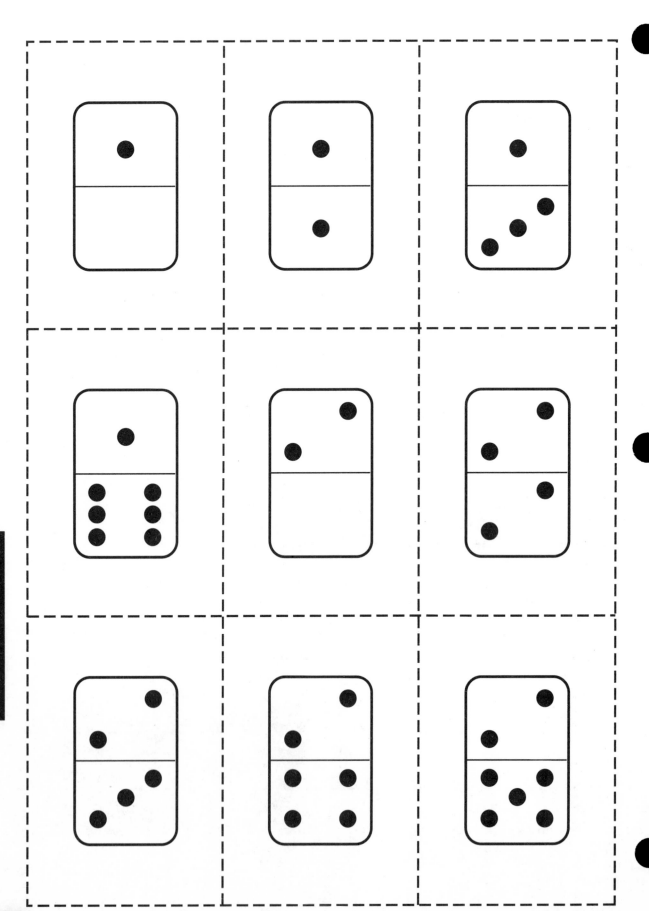

Resources

Domino Cards

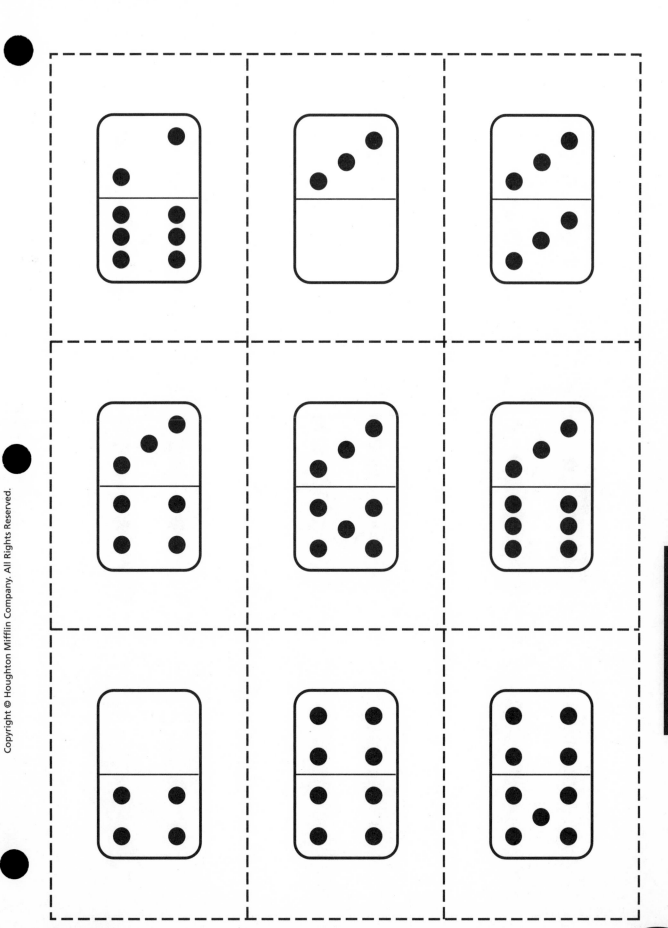

Resources

Domino Cards

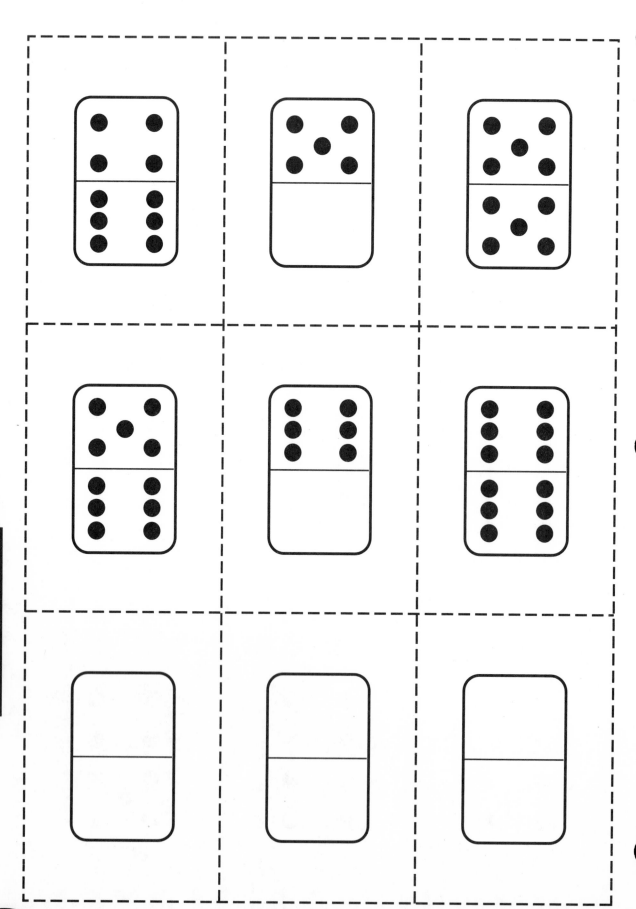

Resources

Domino Cards

Dot Cards

0	1	2
3	4	5
6	7	8

Resources

Number Cards 0–50

9	10	11
12	13	14
15	16	17

Resources

18	19	20
21	**22**	**23**
24	**25**	**26**

Resources

Number Cards 0–50

27	28	29
30	31	32
33	34	35

Resources

36	37	38
39	40	41
42	43	44

Number Cards 0–50

Resources

45	46	47
48	49	50
+	−	=

Resources

51	52	53
54	55	56
57	58	59

Resources

Number Cards 51–100

60	61	62
63	64	65
66	67	68

Resources

69	70	71
72	73	74
75	76	77

Resources

Number Cards 51–100

78	79	80
81	82	83
84	85	86

Resources

87	88	89
90	91	92
93	94	95

Resources

96	97	98
99	100	

Number Cards 51–100

Resources

Playing Card Master

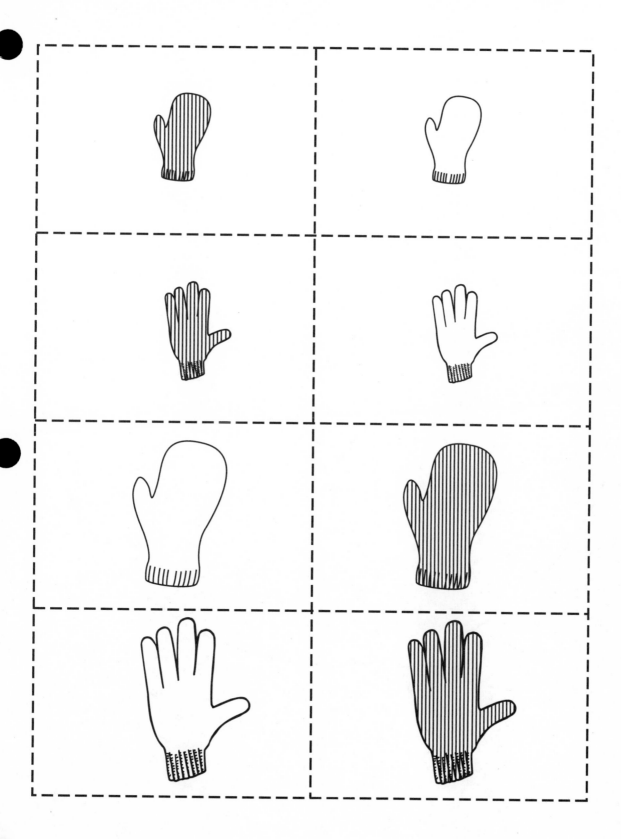

Resources

Sorting Cards

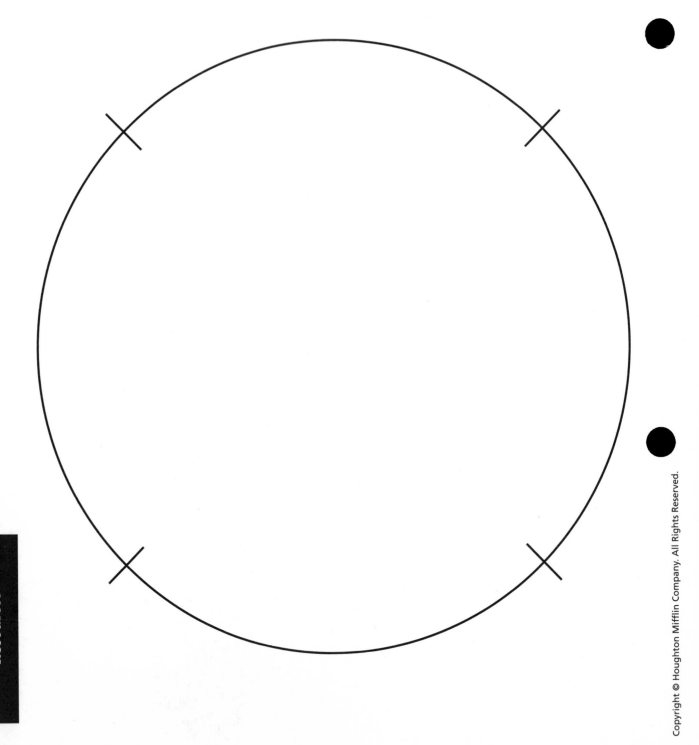

Resources

Blank Spinner

3-Part Spinner

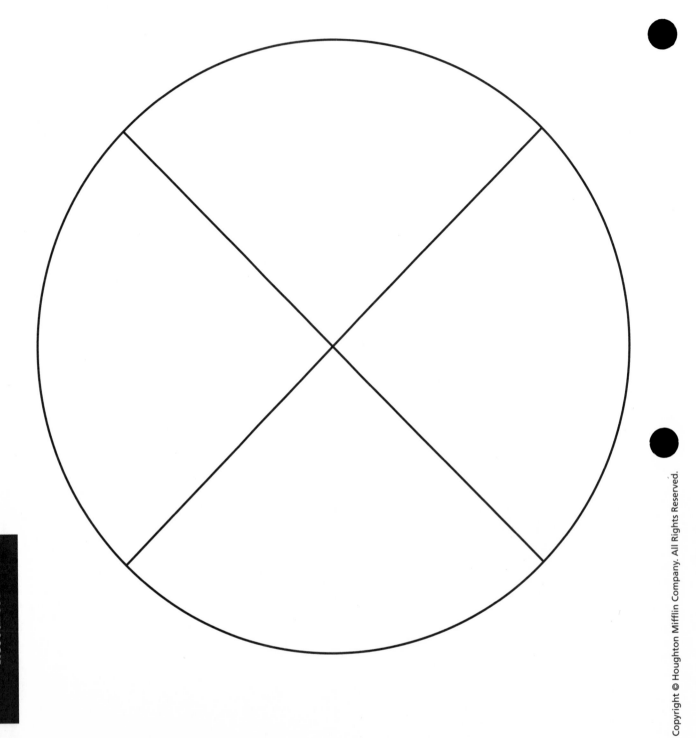

Resources

4-Part Spinner

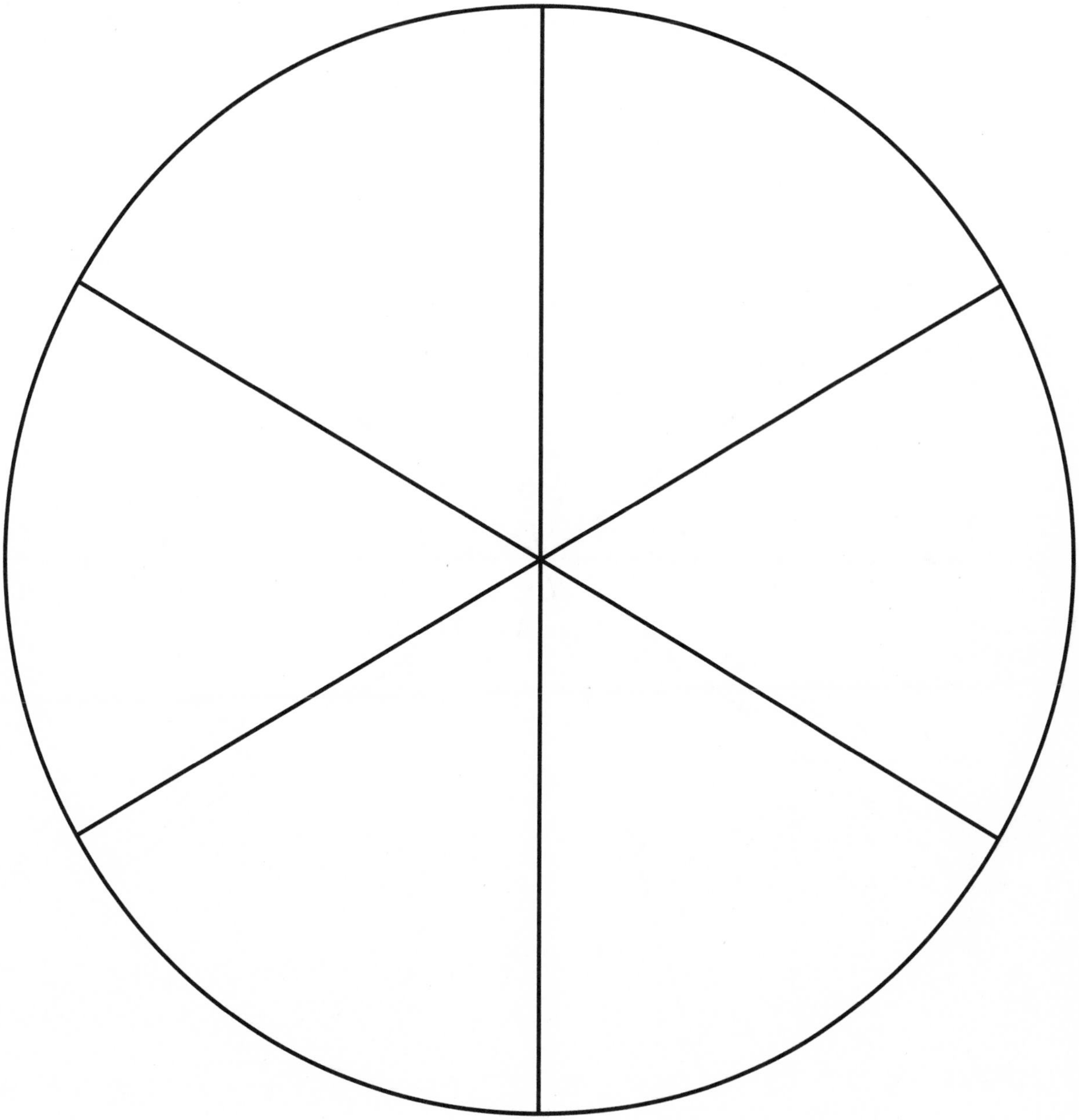

Resources

6-Part Spinner

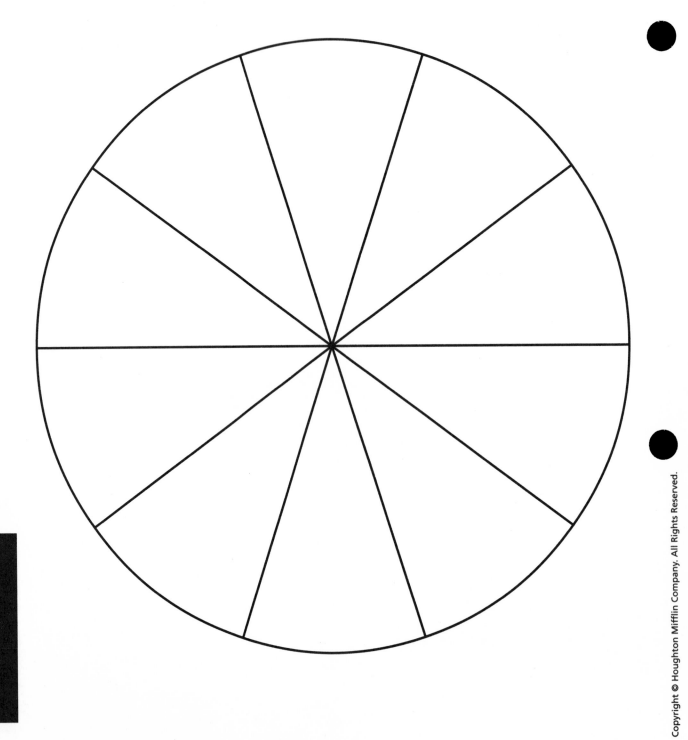

Resources

10-Part Spinner

| 50¢
Half Dollars | 25¢
Quarters | |

Money Workmat

10¢ Dimes	5¢ Nickels	1¢ Pennies

Money Workmat

Whole

Part

Part

Resources

Resources

Ten Frame Workmat

Ten Frame Workmat

Resources

Tens	Ones

Tens and Ones Workmat

Tens and Ones Workmat

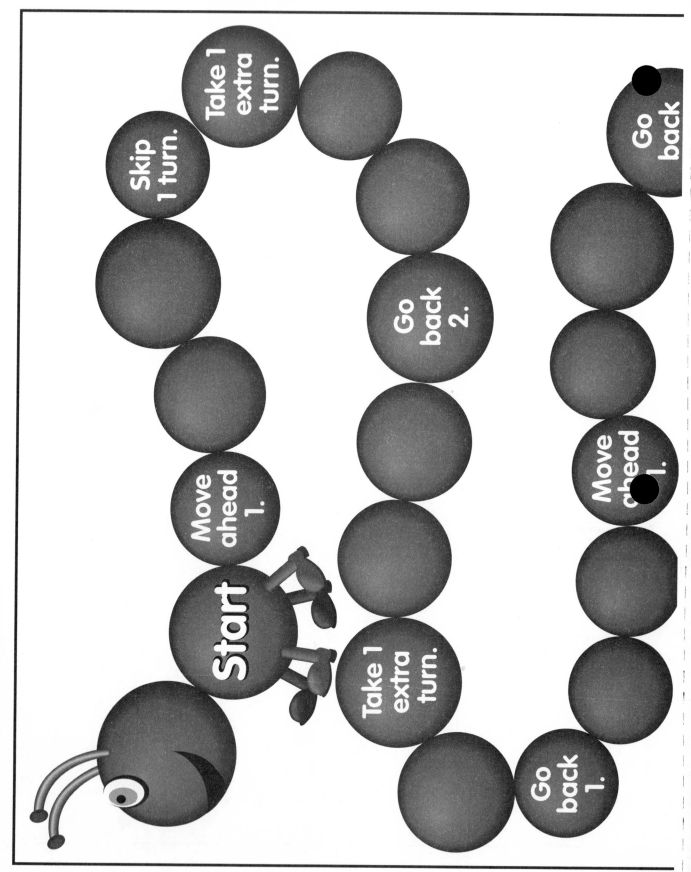

The following text appears on the gameboard spaces:

Skip 1 turn.

Take 1 extra turn.

Go back

Go back 2.

Move ahead 1.

Move ahead 1.

Start

Take 1 extra turn.

Go back 1.

Caterpillar Gameboard

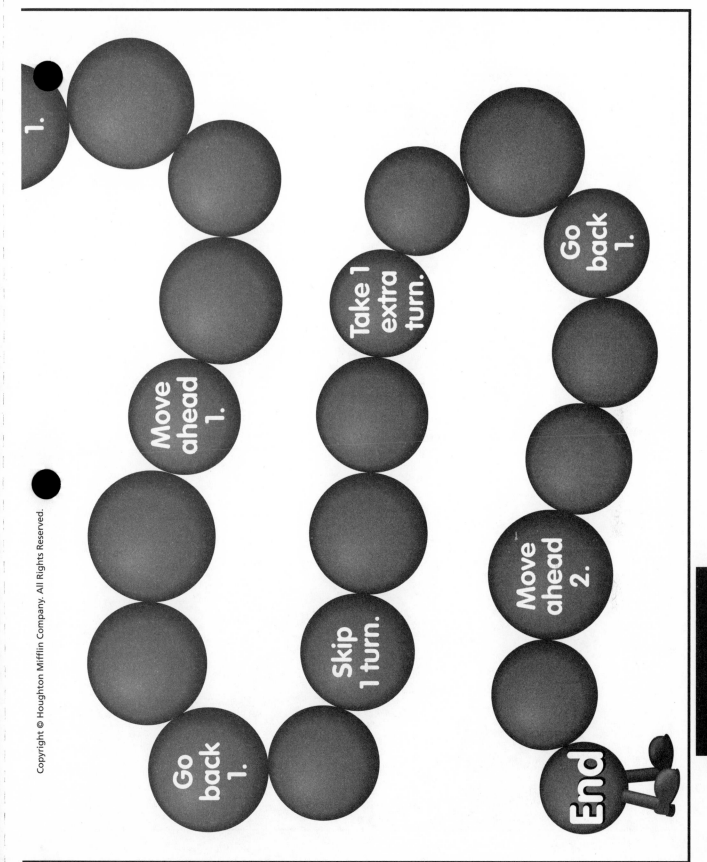

1.

Move ahead 1.

Go back 1.

Skip 1 turn.

Take 1 extra turn.

Go back 1.

Move ahead 2.

End

Caterpillar Gameboard

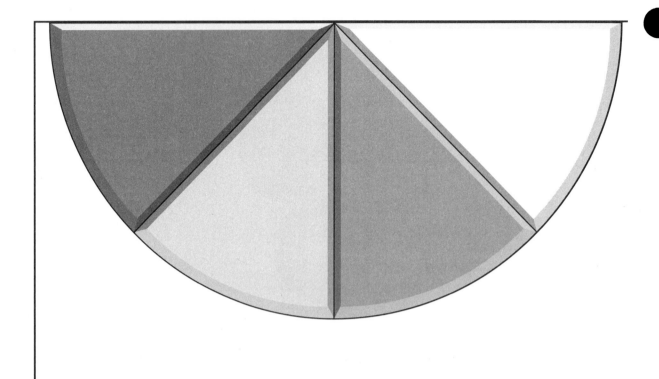

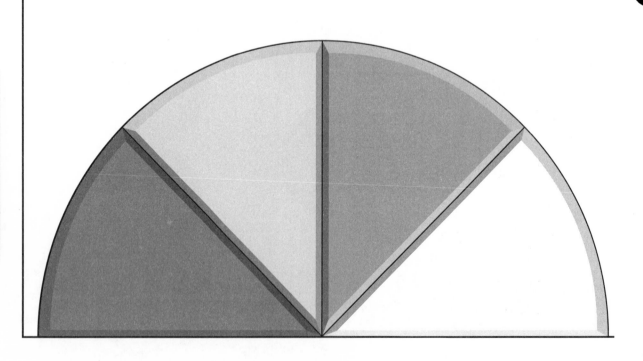

Resources

Fan Gameboard

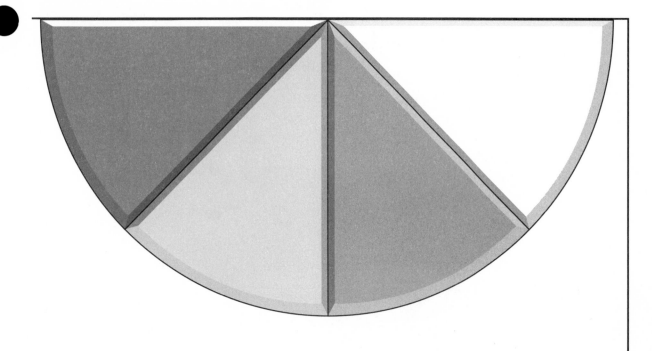

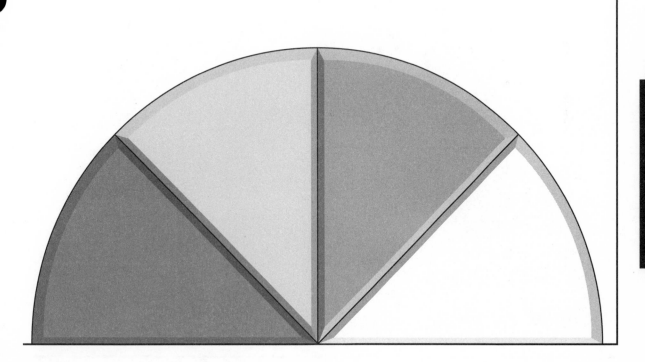

Resources

Fan Gameboard

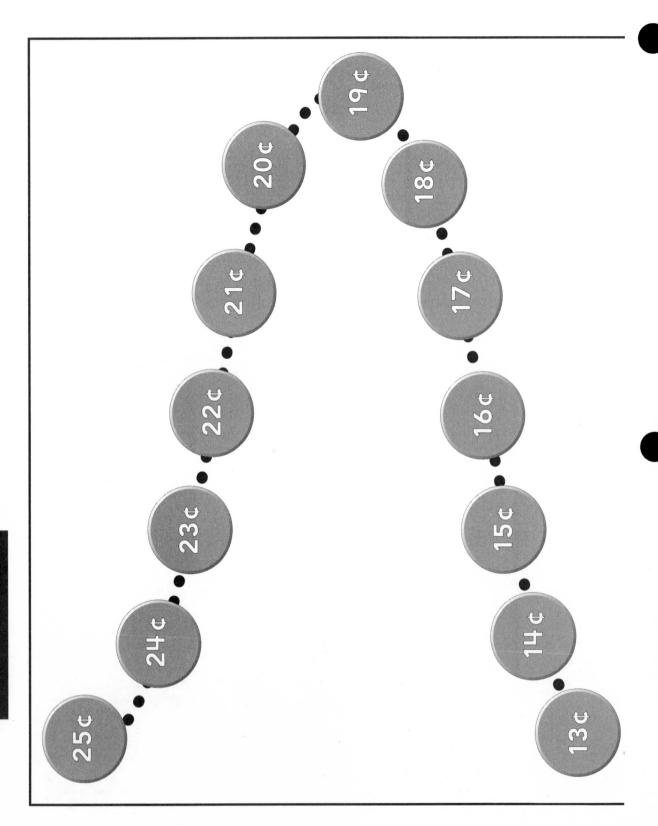

Resources

Great Coin Count Gameboard

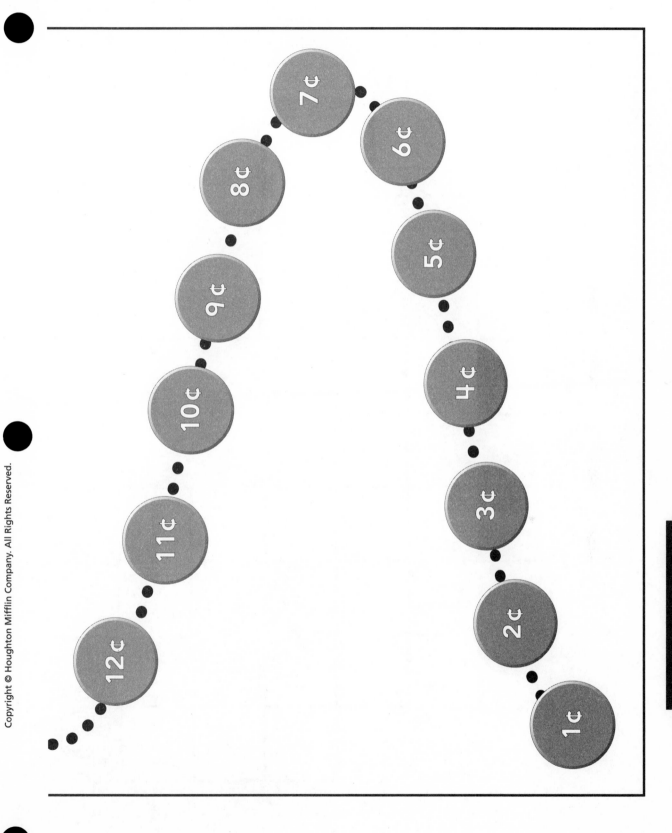

Great Coin Count Gameboard

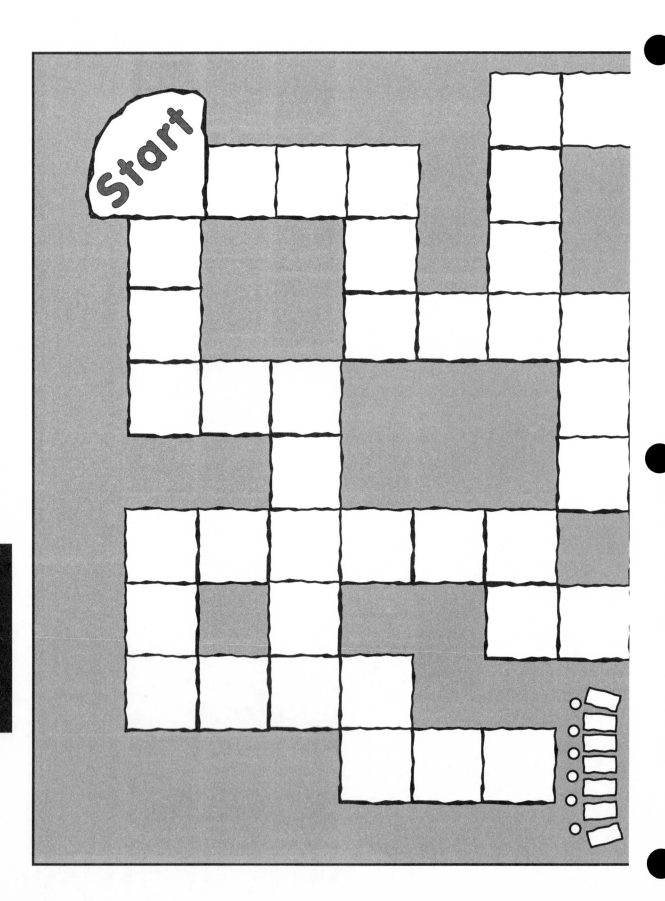

Start

Resources

Maze Gameboard

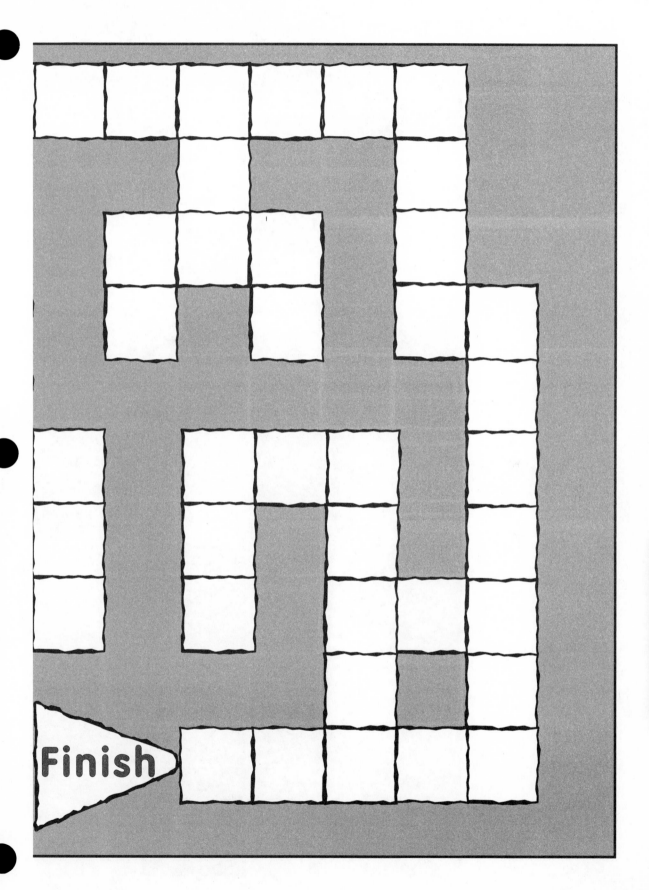

Finish

Maze Gameboard

Resources

Move It! Gameboard

Move It! Gameboard

Resources

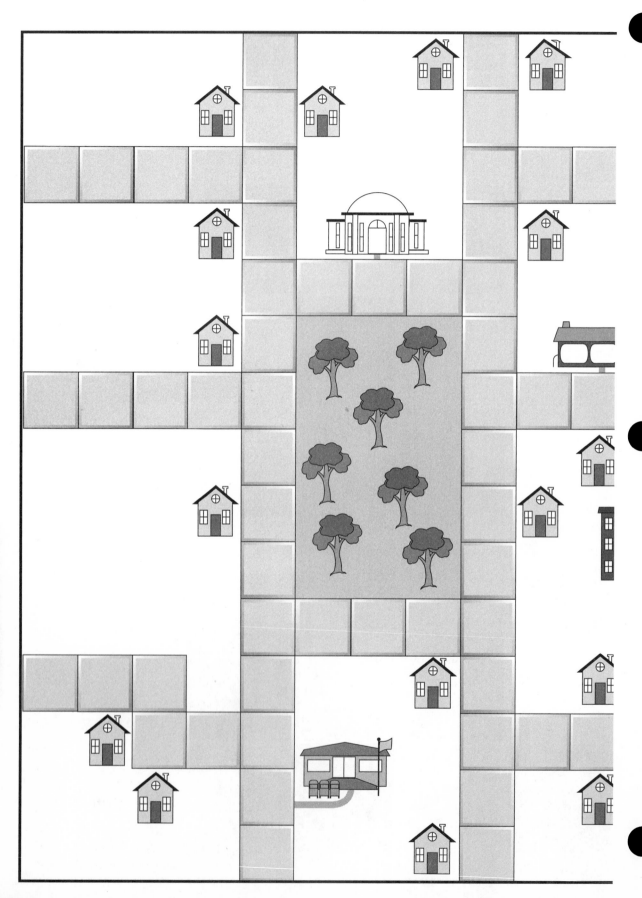

Neighborhood Gameboard

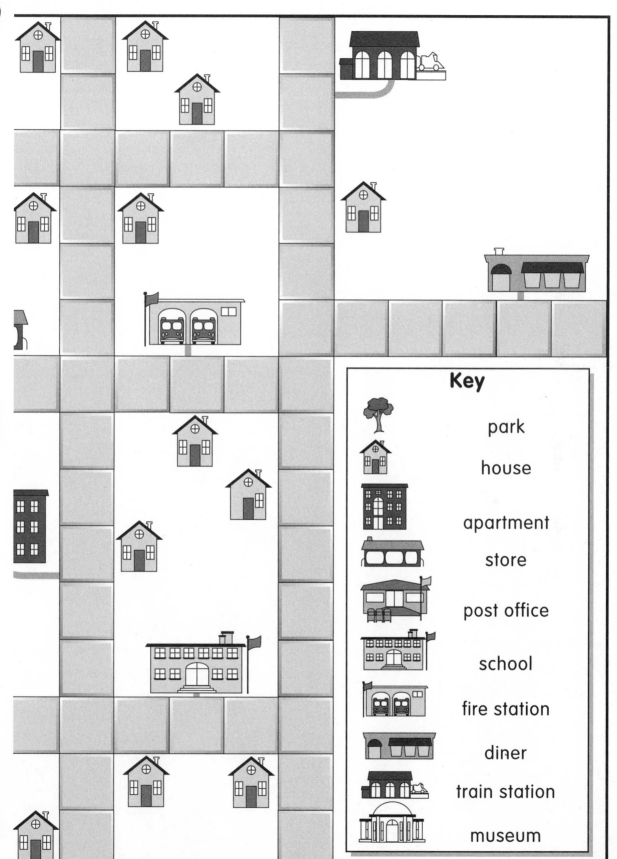

Key

park

house

apartment

store

post office

school

fire station

diner

train station

museum

Resources

Neighborhood Gameboard